"TELL THE WORLD"

"TELL THE WORLD"

WHAT HAPPENED IN CHINA AND WHY

LIU BINYAN

with Ruan Ming and Xu Gang

TRANSLATED BY
HENRY L. EPSTEIN

PANTHEON BOOKS   NEW YORK

Library of Congress Cataloging-in-Publication Data

Liu, Pin-yen, 1925–
    Tell the world : what happened in China and why / Liu Binyan ;
with Ruan Ming and Xu Gang.
    p. cm.
    ISBN 0-394-58370-1
    1. China—History—Tiananmen Square Incident, 1989. I. Ruan, Ming,
1931– . II. Xu, Gang.
    III. Title.
DS779.32.L58 1989
951.05′8—dc20   89-43171

BOOK DESIGN BY CATHRYN S. AISON

Manufactured in the United States of America

FIRST EDITION

"You must tell the world what is happening. Otherwise all this counts for nothing."

STUDENT IN TIANANMEN SQUARE,

June 4, 1989

CONTENTS

PREFACE

This book was written by three people whose ages and backgrounds differ, but whose fates have been similar in the past ten years or so. We all joined the Communist Party of China—one of us during the anti-Japanese War (1937–1945), one during the War of Liberation (1945–1949), one after the founding of the People's Republic of China in 1949. We were all dismissed from the Party at different times and in different fashions.

Only one of us, Xu Gang, participated directly in the 1989 Democracy movement in Beijing. He did not leave Tiananmen Square until the massacre on June 4. But we have all been deeply involved in various ways in analyzing the enormous changes that have swept China in the last decade; and this book draws deeply on our observations of China, from different angles, over the past few decades. Our analysis of China was, and remains, interwoven with our efforts to change our country. In the future, we hope to continue to do our part in ending this current chapter of China's history as soon as possible.

In the speeches that I made in some universities on the West Coast of the United States in the spring of 1988, I said that unexpected events could take place in China at any time, and that China could well become the center of world attention, because 1989 marked the fortieth anniversary of the founding of the PRC, as well as the seventieth anniversary of the May Fourth movement for democracy. The crises and hopes of China would, I said, show themselves on these occasions. China is a country that produces miracles. In 1949 the army, led by the Communist Party, defeated the soldiers of the Kuomintang, who were much better equipped and more numerous than the soldiers of the Party, and won political power. At present, the Chinese on the mainland, in Taiwan and Hong Kong, and all over the world are endeavoring to create another miracle. The three million soldiers now under the Communist Party will ultimately be immobilized without attack by any armed forces. I have said that the nature of what has happened in China is disintegration—disintegration of the old social structure, the old political system, the old social relations, and the old ideology. This process is not yet complete, but the events of June 1989 greatly accelerated the process.

The first part of the book was written by Xu Gang and myself, the second part by Ruan Ming, and the third part by myself.

Liu Binyan

August 25, 1989

A GUIDE TO PEOPLE, INSTITUTIONS, AND EVENTS

PEOPLE

The Gang of the Old

The Gang of the Old is a group of Party stalwarts, not all of whom hold official positions in the national government:

Deng Xiaoping (b. 1904). Paramount leader of China and chairman of the Central Military Commission.

Bo Yibo (b. 1909). A vice-chairman of the Party's Central Advisory Commission, a former Politburo member and vice-premier.

Chen Yun (b. 1905). A Communist Party member since 1925 specializing in financial and economic work. Chairman, Central Advisory Commission.

Li Xiannian (b. 1905). A former Politburo member, finance minister, vice-premier during the Cultural Revolution and president of China, now chairman of the Chinese People's Political Consultative Conference.

Peng Zhen (b. 1902). A former Politburo member and mayor of Beijing; former chairman of the National People's Congress.

Song Renqiong (b. 1909). Vice-chairman of CCP Central Advisory Committee.

Wang Zhen (b. 1909). A veteran army general and conservative stalwart. Vice-premier during the Cultural Revolution and now vice-president of China.

Yang Shangkun (b. 1907). President of the People's Republic and vice-chairman of the Central Military Commission. A former director of the Central Office of the Party.

Standing Committee of Politburo as of April 15, 1989

Hu Qili (b. 1929). In charge of propaganda and ideology before martial law was declared.

Li Peng (b. 1928). Prime minister.

Qiao Shi (b. 1924). Vice-premier, in charge of the nation's public security.

Yao Yilin (b. 1917). Vice-premier; specializes in economics.

Zhao Ziyang (b. 1919). Communist Party general secretary.

Standing Committee of Politburo as of October 1, 1989

Jiang Zemin (b. 1926). Communist Party general secretary.

Li Peng. Prime minister.

Li Ruihuan (b. 1934). Mayor of Tianjin. In charge of propaganda and ideology.

Qiao Shi (b. 1924). Vice-premier; in charge of the nation's public security.

Yao Yilin. Vice-premier.

Beijing Municipal Officials

Chen Xitong (b. 1930). Mayor of Beijing.

Li Ximing (b. 1926). Communist Party secretary of the Beijing Municipal Committee.

INSTITUTIONS

The Communist Party

The *Communist Party (CCP)* exercises the paramount leadership role in the government, the military, and all mass organizations.

The *National Party Congress* is theoretically the most powerful organ of the CCP. Convened every five years, it elects a *Central Committee.*

The *Central Committee* functions as the highest organ of Party authority between congresses. It elects the *Politburo;* when the Central Committee is not in session, the Politburo and its *Standing Committee* exercise its power and functions.

The Government

The *State Council,* headed by the premier, is the largest administrative organ of the Central Government. The premier is nominated by the CCP and approved by the National People's Congress.

The *National People's Congress (NPC)* is elected every five years and theoretically has the power to appoint and remove the premier and other members of the State Council. It also approves the national economic plans and the national budget.

The *Standing Committee of the NPC* is elected by the NPC and functions as a full time organ of the NPC, interpreting laws and enacting decrees.

EVENTS

1919

May 4: Students demonstrations begin May Fourth movement.

1949

October 1: Founding of the People's Republic of China.

1956

Mao Zedong declares, "Let a hundred flowers blossom."

1957

February: Mao calls upon intellectuals to criticize the Chinese Communist Party.

May: Mao calls upon the intellectuals to help the Party's rectification campaign.

June: Antirightist campaign begins, attacking those who had taken part in the Hundred Flowers movement, and those who had criticized the CCP too outspokenly.

1958

The Great Leap Forward.

1959–61

The "three bad years" of economic crisis in the wake of the Great Leap Forward. More than 30 million people die of starvation.

1966

The Cultural Revolution begins.

1971

Lin Biao dies.

1973

August 24–28: At the Tenth Party Congress of the Chinese Communist Party, Deng Xiaoping is reelected to the Central Committee after six years of political exile.

1976

January 8: Premier Zhou Enlai dies.

February 3: Hua Guofeng, the minister of public security, is appointed acting premier.

April 5: Spontaneous demonstrations in memory of Zhou Enlai in Tiananmen Square are suppressed by the Gang of Four, violently.

April 7: The incident in Tiananmen Square is labeled a "counterrevolutionary political incident." Deng Xiaoping is attacked as the instigator of the movement and stripped of all his posts.

September 9: Chairman Mao dies.

October 6: The Gang of Four, including Mao's wife, is arrested. The Cultural Revolution is declared to be at an end.

1977

July 16–21: The Central Committee appoints Hua Guofeng to be Party chairman and premier, while Deng Xiaoping is restored to his posts.

1978

November 19: The first big-character posters appear at Xidan intersection of Beijing—marking the beginning of the Democracy Wall movement.

December 18–22: At the Third Plenary Session of the Central Committee of the Eleventh People's Congress, Deng consolidates his power and announces a new era of economic development.

1979

January 1: US-China normalization takes effect.

January 3: Hu Yaobang is named general secretary of the Communist Party.

January 28: Deng arrives in the United States on a nine-day visit.

February 17: China launches an attack against Vietnam.

March 29: Wei Jingsheng, editor of a dissent magazine and author of the article *The Fifth Modernization: Democracy,* is arrested and denounced as a counterrevolutionary.

March 30: Deng announces that China will modernize within a commitment to the Four Cardinal Principles: socialism, the dictatorship of the proletariat, Party leadership, and Marxism–Leninism–Mao Zedong Thought.

1980

September 7: Hua Guofeng is removed as premier and Zhao Ziyang is named to succeed him.

1981

April: The first campaign against "bourgeois liberalization" criticizing the liberalization in literature and arts.

June 27–29: Hua Guofeng resigns as Party chairman and is succeeded by Hu Yaobang.

1983

October: The start of the second campaign against "bourgeois liberalization," also known as the campaign against "spiritual contamination."

1985

January 1: The publication of Deng Xiaoping's speech advocating an open-door policy for China.

September 18: The students of Beijing University rally to commemorate the fifty-fourth anniversary of the Japanese invasion of China. Following their lead, students in several big cities demonstrate, much against the Party's will, to protest the Japanese economic invasion of China, and the lack of political freedom.

1986

December 5: Demanding better living conditions, democracy, and freedom of the press, students demonstrate at the University of Science and Technology in Hefei, Anhui province.

December 23: Students in Beijing demonstrate, calling for freedom and democracy.

December 31: The Chinese government announces that there is a plot to overthrow the government and places limits on all demonstrations.

1987

January 1: Over two thousand students demonstrate in Beijing in defiance of the new regulations.

January 14, 19, and 24: Fang Lizhi, Wang Ruowang, and Liu Binyan are expelled from the Communist Party and accused of encouraging the student demonstrations. The beginning of the third campaign against "bourgeois liberalization."

January 16: Hu Yaobang is removed as general secretary. Zhao Ziyang is named acting general secretary.

November 11: Li Peng is named acting premier.

1988

March 25: The National People's Congress confirms the appointment of Li Peng. Yang Shangkun is elected president of China and Wan Li is named head of the National People's Congress.

Summer: Unprecedented inflation begins.

September 15–21: The Politburo decides to postpone price reform for at least two years.

September 26–30: The Central Committee supports Premier Li Peng's efforts to slow the pace of economic reform.

1989

April 15: Hu Yaobang dies.

April 16: Thousands of students pour into Tiananmen Square to mourn Hu's death.

April 21–22: Up to a hundred thousand people demonstrate in Tiananmen Square, demanding freedom and democracy.

April 26: The *People's Daily* publishes an editorial calling the student demonstrators a "small bunch of troublemakers," labeling the movement a "counterrevolutionary rebellion," and hinting ominously of a government crackdown.

May 13: Three thousand students begin a hunger strike in Tiananmen Square.

May 15: Mikhail Gorbachev arrives in Beijing.

May 19: A million people take to the streets to support the hunger strikers.

May 20: Martial Law is officially declared by Li Peng "in some parts of Beijing."

June 4: Troops occupy Tiananmen Square.

June 23: The Central Committee meets to strip Zhao Ziyang of his positions, he is replaced by Shanghai Mayor Jiang Zemin.

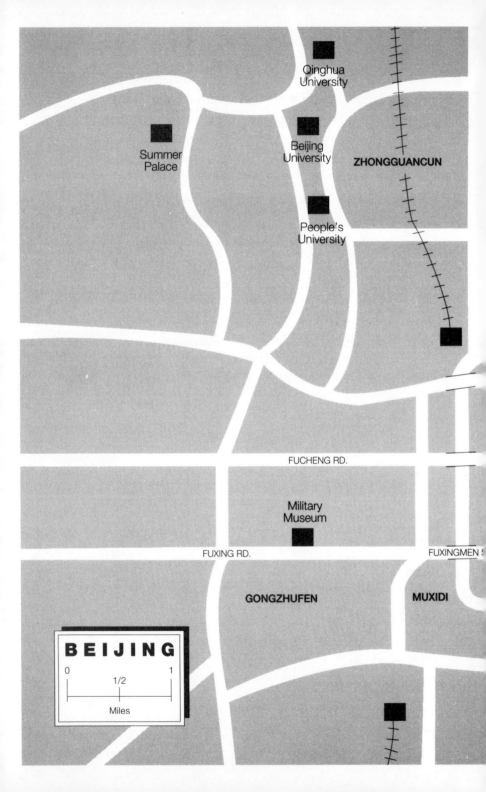

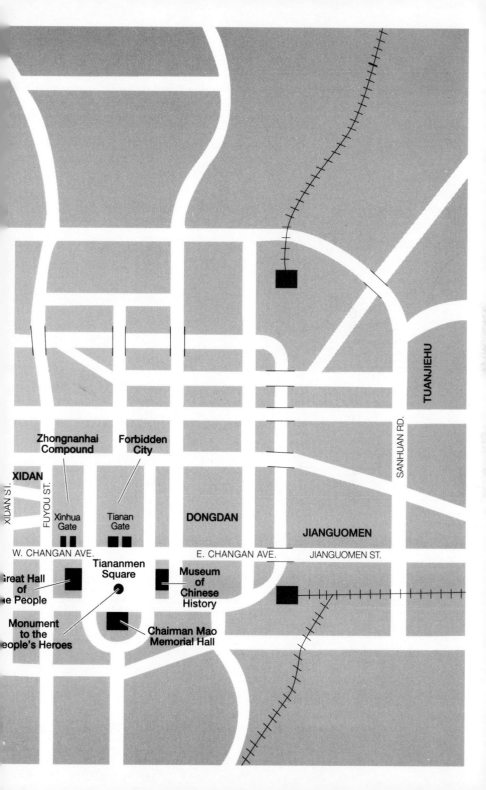

XIDAN

Zhongnanhai
Compound

Forbidden
City

XIDAN ST.

FUYOU ST.

Xinhua
Gate

Tianan
Gate

DONGDAN

JIANGUOMEN

SANHUAN RD.

TUANJIEHU

W. CHANGAN AVE.

E. CHANGAN AVE.

JIANGUOMEN ST.

Great Hall
of
the People

Tiananmen
Square

Museum
of
Chinese
History

Monument
to the
People's Heroes

Chairman Mao
Memorial Hall

1

BEIJING'S UNFORGETTABLE SPRING

Behind thick palace walls, a few old men who thought they could decide China's future were thinking and planning. The old men scarcely knew or cared what the people outside were thinking, worrying and complaining about. And nobody outside knew anything about what went on behind those red walls. No wonder the Chinese themselves rarely know why their lives are so hard, and so unpleasant.

Major events in China often take people by surprise. The old men did not anticipate what was to happen this time. But they were not the only ones; even the participants were surprised by what happened.

———

Two years earlier, at the end of 1986, students at the Chinese University of Science and Technology in Hefei, Anhui Province, had protested against the government's ruling that their election of representatives for the People's Congress was null and void. They took to the streets to demand protection of their right to vote. Then college students from more than a dozen cities, from Heilongjiang Province in the north to Sichuan Province in the south, also took to the streets to demand democracy.

This student movement, involving dozens of cities, shocked Deng Xiaoping and his clique of old men. In a panic, they hurried to wipe out the movement. According to their logic, the only reason students would start a movement was that they had too much freedom, not too little. The Gang of the Old blamed Hu Yaobang, then general secretary of the Communist Party, for they had long been convinced that Hu was an agent of "bourgeois liberalization." The problem seemed easy to solve: they forced Hu to resign and ousted a few intellectuals, elements of "liberalization," from the Party—that's all.

At the time, it seemed to work. The campuses became quieter. Students seemed to have lost their spirit. They played mah-jongg, danced, dated. Some even left school to enter business. Party officials did not worry about the students. Whatever they do, it's all right, as long as they stay out of politics, they thought. Other students buried themselves in books, especially English books, trying to pass the necessary examinations to go abroad.

In the eyes of Chinese outside the campuses, the students were a failed generation. They had lost hope in China's future. They were disillusioned and would never go into the streets to demonstrate. This view reinforced the common argument

4

that China has no future. However, between 1987 and 1989, the campuses began to make noise. In many universities, "salons" sprang up, as students discussed China's problems. This the Party did not welcome. Government agents quietly observed, and made notes on the personalities, speeches, and actions of student leaders, so that some day they could be dealt with. A few incidents sent chills down official spines: for instance, one student at Beijing University and one from the Language Institute were killed by thugs. These were actually criminal cases. Why then did students go on strike in response? Why did they take to the streets? What were the deeper political forces at work here? But these incidents too were eventually smoothed over after some persuasion.

THE GATHERING STORM

There were times when political issues were raised directly. At the beginning of 1988, a *dazibao,* a "big-character poster" appeared at Beijing University. It raised three questions: What did Li Peng achieve at the Ministry of Water and Power* and on the State Education Commission? For what accomplishments did Li Peng become premier of the State Council? If Li Peng was qualified, what other Chinese was not?

Chinese students believed Li Peng was incompetent. As chairman of the State Education Commission, Li Peng did nothing when rising educational costs and the need to improve the treatment of intellectuals became pressing issues, while the Chinese education budget expenditure per capita fell to the second lowest in the world. Now, this person was going to be

*The ministry in charge of dams, irrigating water, and hydroelectricity.

5

premier of the State Council. How could the students help but be furious?

This poster, like other posters that caused the government worry, was torn down soon after it appeared on the wall. But the officials carefully preserved the handwriting on the poster so that they could trace the person who wrote it. No one knew that this poster represented the wishes of so many people, or knew how to dispel the feelings of discontent and resentment. Typically, the government thought that suppressing expressions of discontent would bring peace.

The year 1989 was an unusual year. There were three major anniversaries: the two hundredth anniversary of the French Revolution, the seventieth anniversary of the May Fourth movement, and the fortieth anniversary of the founding of the People's Republic of China. The relationship among these three anniversaries also stirred emotions. Why has China still not achieved the ideals advocated by the French Revolution—freedom, equality, and fraternity—goals announced by the United Nations human-rights manifesto? In the seventy years since the May Fourth movement, the Chinese have sacrificed so much. Why then have the Chinese people not only failed to achieve more democracy, but been subjected to autocratic rule in the name of revolution? Democratic trends over the world, especially those within the Soviet Union and in many countries of Eastern Europe, were all prompting Chinese intellectuals to take action.

In February 1989, Beijing witnessed an unusual incident. Fang Lizhi wrote a letter to Deng Xiaoping, hoping that he would follow the trend of respecting human rights and release Wei Jingsheng, who had been arrested for demanding democracy and had been in prison for ten years. Following Fang

Lizhi's letter, thirty-three intellectuals wrote an open letter to the Central Committee and the State Council, asking them to release Wei, who had been arrested for political crimes in 1979. Among those who signed the letters were intellectuals who had heretofore shown little interest in politics. Using the form of an open letter demonstrated that these people no longer trusted the Communist Party. They were publicizing their demands to the whole world, and demanding something that was unacceptable to Deng Xiaoping. Ten years earlier, Deng had already concluded: Once we capture Wei Jingsheng, we will never release him! The open letter showed contempt for Deng Xiaoping. When since 1949 have Chinese intellectuals been so bold? So the government moved to dilute the influence of this letter. Officials sought out each of the signers for "private talks," to try to change their attitudes. Just at this juncture, a second open letter appeared. Forty-two scientists and social scientists—all prominent and none typically concerned with politics—signed. This was followed by a third open letter, signed by young writers and scholars and making more extensive demands for democracy.

This was in fact a very important signal. But it was not perceived correctly. As in the past, the recipients took the letters as a challenge to their authority, a demonstration of hostility. They felt that "the fact that we did not arrest the petitioners or pay attention to the letters was already lenient enough."

ONE PERSON'S DEATH

April 15, 1989, was an ordinary night. People were sitting in front of their television sets. For Beijing residents, it was a half-hour of news. People all wanted to know what was happening and what was going to happen.

Funeral music sounded. The Chinese had expected this music. After the music, a portrait of Hu Yaobang appeared on the screen in a black frame. Hu Yaobang was dead. On that evening, Beijing was truly silent. People were silently angry: Damn, they thought, the one who should not die has died.

The same evening, in the triangular plaza of Beijing University—a place where students exchanged opinions—poetry and couplets mourning and commemorating Hu were posted. The next day, students and teachers of Beijing University, Qinghua University, Beijing Normal University, Beijing Institute of Politics and Law, and the People's University simultaneously changed the memorials for Hu Yaobang into sessions criticizing corruption and bureaucracy in the Party. Qinghua University was the first to demand that Li Peng resign. The couplet presented by Beijing University said: "The one who should not die, died. Those who should die live." Overnight, it spread throughout Beijing.

Around eight o'clock on April 17, Wang Dan, initiator of the democratic group in Beijing University, made a speech commemorating Hu Yaobang. After it, he was surrounded by students. Zhang Boli, poet and student writer at Beijing University, made a proposal: Shall we demonstrate on the campus? Amid a burst of enthusiasm, led by Wang Dan, about a hundred students started off from the plaza and marched around the Nameless Lake, shouting slogans commemorating Hu Yaobang.

This group very quickly became an army of more than five thousand. The campus had become too small to contain so many students. They decided to march to Tiananmen Square. They did, shouting, "Down with bureaucracy!" "Long live democracy!" "Hu Yaobang will never die!" The sound first woke the people living in Zhongguancun, the university residential area; then it woke people around the overpass* at Fuxingmen. Going by way of Changan Avenue—the Avenue of Eternal Peace—it finally reached the heart of Beijing—Tiananmen Square, the Square at the Gate of Heavenly Peace. The Democracy movement had begun.

April 18 dawned windless and sunny. The early light revealed the demonstrators in Tiananmen Square. There were more than a hundred thousand students from more than a dozen universities and colleges, as well as other people who had gathered in the half-mile-long square to make various demands of the government:

1. Reevaluate Hu Yaobang's achievements.
2. Reject the campaigns against "spiritual contamination" and "bourgeois liberalization," and rehabilitate Fang Lizhi, Wang Ruowang, and Liu Binyan.
3. Reveal the true financial situation of Party and state leaders, as well as that of their children.
4. Allow freedom of the press; lift censorship of newspapers.
5. Increase funds for education; improve the treatment of intellectuals.
6. Cancel Beijing's ten regulations against demonstrations.
7. Allow the public to know about the development of the student movement.

*Central Beijing is surrounded by a ring road; the major avenues cross it on overpasses and connect with it by ramps

When the people of Beijing bicycled to work that morning as usual, they were delighted to discover that students were on the streets. They then passed information about the demonstration on to others.

There was hope for the dismissal of corrupt officials!

There was hope for structural reform!

There was hope for China!

People thought so and said so.

Beijing had a festive atmosphere. Residents gathered at a few main intersections and stood on tiptoe to get a better view. Even peddlers, usually very shrewd and businesslike, were giving students whole cartons of sodas, saying, "What can the students get out of this? They are only trying to speak for us!" Somehow, the students had touched a nerve.

The students for their part were immensely buoyed by the support of the people and by the fact that they had broken the Municipal Committee's ten regulations restricting demonstrations. But from the outset, the students were rational, calm, even discreet. In order to avoid conflict with the government and the police, they always had their own guard lines, walking with linked arms on either side of the main march. They obeyed and sometimes even helped traffic police with traffic control.

Meanwhile, in order to win sympathy from more Beijing residents, the students also broadened the appeal of their slogans. They posted slogans like "Stop politicians from engaging in illegal trade!" and "Eliminate corruption!" in more obvious places, further strengthening the connection with the people. Wherever the parade went, residents shouted, "Long live the students!" The students shouted, "Long live the people!"

This bond between students and residents characterized the

movement from the very start. And once started, the movement acquired its own dynamic.

On the morning of April 19, almost ten thousand students marched to Xinhua Gate, the front gate of Zhongnanhai, where the government leaders live. They were chased away by the police. At ten o'clock in the evening, students once again approached the gate and shouted: "Come out, Li Peng!"

Li Peng would not come out. The wall—with "Serve the People" carved in huge characters—blocked the people's view.

Early on the morning of April 20, five thousand students gathered in front of the Xinhua Gate. Again and again they shouted, asking the government officials to join them in a dialogue. What they got instead were beatings by the police. Several thousand military police used belts and heavy boots to beat and kick the students. According to Zhang Boli, the student poet, more than three thousand students were kicked or beaten; many fell to the ground and then were beaten even more. Wang Dan, standing on the back of a bicycle, organized the retreat. But the five thousand who retreated to Tiananmen Square had no way to escape. Only because the sun was rising and the police brutality would have been exposed in daylight were the students able to break out of the encirclement. It was a blood-tainted dawn.

ANOTHER KIND OF MOURNING

On April 20, after the students were beaten in Tiananmen Square, they organized into small groups and went into the streets to make speeches to the people. The main themes of these speeches were: Why are we demonstrating? Why are we petitioning the government? Where is China going? Why is corruption so hard to fight? The speakers also gave a detailed account of how the beating took place.

A fundraising drive began to help care for the students who had been injured and to feed the rest. Residents of Beijing came to the students to deliver money. People came all the way from the eastern suburbs to give money to students in Zhongguancun. Although plagued by price increases, Beijing residents still managed to take 10, 50, or 100 yuan from their paychecks, and give it to the students. Once, when the students refused to take one worker's donation saying, "This is your whole month's pay!" the donor replied, with tears in his eyes, "This is not money. This is our conscience!"

Hu Yaobang's memorial ceremony was to be held in the Great Hall of the People, on Tiananmen Square on April 22. On the evening of April 21, Beijing TV announced a curfew in Tiananmen Square and the area around Xinhua Gate from eight to twelve on April 22. Fundraising and speeches were forbidden.

Millions of angry people sat in front of their television sets. Every Chinese knows that Deng Pufang, Deng Xiaoping's son, is the chairman of the Welfare Committee for the Handicapped, and has raised funds at home and abroad. If Deng Pufang could raise funds, why not students? "Why do we need a curfew for the memorial meeting in front of the Great Hall of the People?" Following the example from Beijing University, students at more than a dozen universities and colleges announced that they were on strike. While Beijing TV threatened students and civilians, and people in Beijing were worried that the students would suffer, the students themselves were quietly gathering in Tiananmen Square. They intended to sit

12

there through the whole night on April 21, and on the next morning demand that public memorial ceremonies for Hu Yaobang be permitted.

In the afternoon of April 21, a freshman at Beijing Normal University, Wuer Kaixi, distributed a pamphlet announcing the establishment of an interim student association. By nine o'clock at night, more than forty thousand students and teachers who had collected at Beijing Normal University had set off for Tiananmen Square. Qinghua University students entered the square first. The government, unprepared, had nothing to say. By midnight, about two hundred thousand students and teachers had gathered in the square. Led by Wang Dan, Wuer Kaixi, Zhou Yongjun, and Zhang Boli, the students were in effective control of the square. In order to prevent any incidents that would give the government an excuse to crack down, anyone who had no student ID card was denied entry to the square. People sent food to the students. After midnight, students inside the square settled down. In front of Tianan Gate were armed police. The first all-night sit-in had begun.

April in Beijing is chilly. The two hundred thousand students, sitting on the ground, sang the "Internationale" to fight off the cold. "This is the last struggle—Unite to welcome tomorrow!" they sang. In the still of the night, under the stars, the square was like an open field. The students sat throughout the night and saw the dawn of April 22.

Inside the Great Hall of the People, the official memorial meeting for Hu Yaobang was being held. Yang Shangkun was in charge of the meeting. Those who attended showed no emotion. Deng Xiaoping attended.

And there was Li Peng. Did he hear the students shout,

"Come out, Li Peng!"? Did those inside know that right at this moment, two hundred thousand students were sitting in Tiananmen Square? Yang Shangkun shouted, "Play the 'Internationale'!"—instead of calling for the National Anthem, as he should have. After the meeting was over, Li Peng followed Deng as they left the hall. At the northern gate, they got into their limousines and were carried away.

Meanwhile, five student representatives (later three) were kneeling in front of the Great Hall of the People, handing in their letter of appeal, asking Li Peng to meet the students. They knelt for forty minutes. But the gate was closed, and Li Peng was gone. Even the students' request that the car carrying Hu Yaobang's body make one circuit of Tiananmen Square— which is what usually happens—was denied. The government was afraid of both the dead and the living.

About a million people stood in reverent silence along either side of Western Changan Avenue. These people, who wanted a last look at Hu Yaobang, were weeping.

DENG XIAOPING—THE ARSONIST

Since the beginning of the student movement, the Beijing Municipal Committee had been very busy. Various factions within the Central Committee also sent secret agents to the universities and to Tiananmen Square to collect intelligence.

Li Ximing, head of the Beijing Municipal Committee of the Communist Party, and Chen Xitong, mayor of Beijing, repeatedly appealed to Party leaders, saying that if the Municipal Committee was given the power, it would be able to handle the movement. Power here meant military force. Li Ximing and Chen Xitong would play an important role at this critical

14

historical juncture. Peng Zhen, who had been mayor of Beijing for a long time before the Cultural Revolution, was now an important member of the Gang of the Old. Under his influence, the Beijing Municipal Committee has been on the side of the conservatives for the past ten years. Li Ximing and Li Peng, the premier, had been students together in the Soviet Union, and later had been coworkers in the Beijing Electric Power Bureau. So they cooperated in suppressing the student movement.

The Beijing Municipal Committee drafted a report that contained a distorted and harshly critical account of the student movement, and handed it to the Central Committee. On April 24, the Standing Committee of the Politburo met, and later the entire Politburo. Zhao Ziyang, general secretary of the Party, was absent; this was the second day of his visit to North Korea. And it is worth noting that Bao Tong, political secretary of the Standing Committee, was not allowed to attend the meetings; he had always been considered a close follower of Zhao Ziyang. This move indicated that Zhao was already considered an outsider, to be treated with caution.

At the meetings, those present listened to the report of the Beijing Municipal Committee, decided on a hard-line policy against the student movement, and empowered the Municipal Committee to carry it out. On April 25, on the basis of the Beijing report, Yang Shangkun and Li Peng reported to Deng about the student movement. Deng characterized it this way: "It is a planned conspiracy, a political rebellion." "We will not have a moment's rest if we do not stop it." "We should try to avoid bloodshed. It is hard to shed no blood at all. Don't be afraid of international public opinion." For the first time, Deng Xiaoping revealed his actual intent.

15

One day later, on April 26, an editorial appeared in the *People's Daily*. The title was "Resolutely Oppose Rebellion." It said: "After the memorial meeting, a small handful of people with evil intentions took advantage of people's feelings for Hu Yaobang, and created rumors to confuse people." "They openly violate the Constitution, and encourage opposition to the Communist Party and the socialist system." "This is a planned conspiracy, a rebellion. Its essence is to negate the Communist Party, and to negate the socialist system. This is a major political struggle for the whole Party, and for people of all nationalities in China."

It repeated Deng Xiaoping's words, and labeled the student movement a "counterrevolutionary rebellion." The editorial was broadcast on the radio. People in Beijing were astounded: How could the leadership be so unreasonable? One editorial ignited a conflagration. People sighed, "The Communist Party is forcing people to take to the streets again!"

On the morning of April 27, students at Beijing University started a march and appealed for peace. They went with a deep sense of foreboding. Many had already written their wills. The professors swarmed at the gate, tears flowing down their faces, pleading with the students not to take chances. Citizens cheered the students and protected them from the police. For the editorial smelled of gunpowder. And everyone knew that the Communist Party was the group that had the guns.

Without access to mass media, the students had to pass on information by word of mouth. On the morning of April 27, only one sentence was being passed around: "Students are on the streets, and the military are ready to take action!" People came out of their houses and offices. All the major intersections, such as Xidan, Liubukou, and Dongdan, were heavily guarded. Row upon row of armed police and public-security police stood shoulder to shoulder, their faces expressionless.

As the first part of the parade arrived at Liubukou, shouting, "The People's Liberation Army loves the people!" and pushing the military police aside, the police were also pushing. Nobody wanted to be the first to raise a hand. The police formation was moving nervously, trying to break up the students and then encircle them. The bystanders saw this very clearly. Taking advantage of the fact that they clearly outnumbered the police, they broke up the police the same way. Then they shrank the encirclements, leaving a passage for the students, shouting, "Hurry, pass!" The police line was broken.

At that moment, there was only one slogan: "No use of force! Chinese do not beat Chinese!" People's eyes were fixed on the hands of police. When one policeman started to wipe the sweat off his forehead, a burst of shouted slogans frightened him and he put down his hand. There were also hundreds of cameras. Reporters who volunteered to work among the students and people had just one mission: to record both the great and the evil deeds in the book of history.

What excited the whole of China during the April 27 demonstration was the fact that there were two hundred thousand students in the procession, and over a million workers, intellectuals, and other civilians who made way for them, hailed them, and gave them food and drink.

Before the beginning of the demonstration, some troops of the Thirty-Eighth Army had already entered Beijing. They saw that the students were peaceful and could not bring themselves to attack. The information circulating was that the reason the highest authority could not order suppression was precisely because a million people supported the students. The government had never expected this to happen; it had thought the editorial and the show of force would make people submit. But the government was mistaken; the Chinese people were clearly fed up.

At seven in the evening of April 27, the demonstrators gathered in Tiananmen Square and marched east. Passing under the Jianguomen Overpass, they marched back toward the universities. The people lining the streets, who were applauding them, refused to go home. They waited for the students at every corner, and congratulated them on their victory, their hands filled with gifts of food and drink.

Meanwhile, on the Jianguomen Overpass, a troop transport full of soldiers was stopped in the middle of the road, blocked by the people. This was the first incident of blocking military vehicles. Even when the students had disappeared from view and night was falling, people still refused to let the army vehicle go. "It will catch up with the students!" they said.

At the same time, students in Shanghai, Wuhan, and Changsha also took to the streets, in response to the Beijing students' actions. Shanghai students carried huge banners reading: "RETURN THE WORLD ECONOMIC HERALD!" "RETURN QIN BENLI!"* They passed Nanjing Road and gathered in front of the city

---

*The *World Economic Herald* is a liberal weekly journal published in Shanghai. It had offended the antireform forces in the Party because it used bold language to discuss major political and economic issues. During the antiliberalization movement in 1987 it would have been closed down, had it not been for the protection of Zhao Ziyang. In April 1989, Jiang Zemin, secretary of the Shanghai Municipal Committee, announced at a meeting to report Deng's speech that "work groups" sent by the committee would enter the Shanghai offices of the *Herald* to "rectify" it. Editor-in-chief Qin Benli was suspended and examined. This move aroused longlasting protest and discontent among students and journalists throughout China.

government building at Waitan. The cry for democracy and freedom reverberated throughout China!

The demonstration of April 27 apparently shocked the government, and the leaders felt they had to make some gesture of reconciliation. On April 29, Yuan Mu, spokesman for the State Council, was empowered by Li Peng to talk with forty-five students from the sixteen colleges and universities in Beijing. The student representatives were invited by the two government-run student associations—the National Student Association and the Beijing Student Association.

Was this a real dialogue? Before he entered the room, Wuer Kaixi was told that he could represent only himself, not the independent Interim Student Association of Beijing Colleges and Universities, of which he was chairman. He immediately refused to participate, and announced to the reporters: "This is not the kind of dialogue Beijing students hoped for!"

In the meeting hall, He Dongchang, the chairman of the State Education Commission, a notorious conservative whom the students despised, sat on the dais, looking both condescending and authoritative. Yuan Mu announced that the government would not enter into negotiations with the students. His arrogant remarks irritated not only the students, but also the people of Beijing. There were many microphones in front of Yuan Mu; the students had only one. They were not given a chance to speak even after they had raised their hands many times.

Yuan Mu and He Dongchang also mentioned several times that there were people "behind the students"—"someone with a long beard," "people like Fang Lizhi." Through these remarks, they revealed their real intent. What surprised the people in front of the television sets even more was that when one student presented a magazine with a photograph of Zhao Ziyang playing golf and asked about "a certain leader" playing golf every week, Yuan Mu quickly accepted this question and promised to "pass it on to relevant leaders." Afterward, reporters learned that before this student entered the room, he was given a magazine by someone who looked like a cadre and who disappeared after he thrust this "weapon" into the student's hands.

To comfort the students, Yuan Mu passed on Li Peng's words, saying that what the *People's Daily* editorial contained about the attack on the Communist Party leadership and socialist system was not aimed at students. Talking about freedom of the press, he said, as if the students were idiots, "In our country, there is no censorship system for the media. Our system is that the editors-in-chief of newspapers and magazines have complete responsibility." And, "The so-called censorship of newspapers does not exist. Our media enjoy the freedom described in the Constitution."

Needless to say, the students were dissatisfied with this speech. The Interim Student Association of Beijing Colleges and Universities did not recognize this dialogue as a real one, and asked the Party and government leaders to conduct direct, equal, and substantial dialogues with student "dialogue groups." What the students wanted was real dialogue. The government just wanted to stall for time.

On May 2, the dialogue delegation from the Beijing universities and colleges, led by Wang Dan, handed in an appeal and plan for the dialogues to the Standing Committee of the People's Congress and the Office of the State Council. On

May 3, Yuan Mu held a press conference. He refused to accept the students' plan and repeated his earlier point, "Students cannot talk with the government on an equal basis!" As the spokesman for and representative of the Li Peng government, Yuan Mu played a key role in irritating the students and forcing them to take to the streets again. The popular view of the movement was, "It was all caused by the Communist Party."

THE ROLE OF THE INTELLECTUALS

On May 4, 1919, Beijing University students and intellectuals gathered in Tiananmen Square to protest the Beiyang warlord government's acquiescence in the Versailles Treaty and to demonstrate in favor of more democratic rights for the people—the beginning of the May Fourth movement. Seventy years later, on this May 4, Beijing students again took to the streets, but now it was from the Communist Party that they were demanding more democratic rights. Ever since the Party was established, it has considered itself the successor of the May Fourth movement. But after forty years of this government, the Chinese people have less democracy and freedom—and not more.

A constant stream of people trickled into Tiananmen Square on this morning. The two hundred thousand students who had started from the east and the west entered the square to cheers. They announced a May Fourth Manifesto demanding further dialogue with the government. They also announced that they would resume classes on May 5.

For the first time, students saw another ally join their ranks—the journalists. This student movement, like the one of 1986 and 1987, had demanded that the media report truthfully what was happening, without distortion or slander. And now a new and striking banner read: "THE MEDIA MUST SPEAK THE TRUTH. DO NOT FORCE US TO FABRICATE RUMORS!" Under the banners marched more than five hundred editors and reporters who, for the first time in forty years, decided on their own to join the ranks of the demonstrators.

The greater significance of this event was that for the past forty years the main method used by the Communist Party to control people's minds was to have the media create rumors, fabricate falsehoods, and block real information. Journalists themselves were among the most closely controlled and severely persecuted groups. On this day, there were some old editors and reporters in the ranks who had been labeled "rightists" during the antirightist movement in 1957 for writing truthful reports about China or opposing false reports. They lost the best years of their lives to persecution. Others were persecuted during the Cultural Revolution.

The Communist Party's suppression of free association and the press exceeded that of the Beiyang warlords seventy years ago. If people had not had freedom of the press then, *New Youth,* a journal that spread ideas of democracy, would not have been published; if people had not had freedom of assembly and association, they would not have had the May Fourth movement. At that time, many organizations of different sorts appeared. Now, such organizations were illegal!

The main force in favor of freedom of the press consisted of young and middle-aged editors and reporters. They had less of a burden of tradition and a more rebellious spirit than the older ones, who had been through more periods of political persecution. In recent years, despite the many Party campaigns to oppose "bourgeois liberalization," many newspapers that had been closely controlled by the government had won more freedom. This was due entirely to the efforts of their editors and reporters, who had struggled to break through all kinds of barriers. Now, a more serious struggle was going on in the editorial departments of many newspapers and of the TV and radio stations. Within days, even more barriers would be broken. Among the demonstrators, many of the editors and reporters were Party members; some were even senior members. The fact that they went into the streets showed that they had broken openly with the conservative forces represented by Deng Xiaoping.

When people look back on the Democracy movement, one question will cause debate: What role did the intellectuals play in the movement? Did they do all they could? By the end of April, intellectuals in Beijing already faced an inescapable choice: to plunge into this movement or run away from it. From the beginning, many people had sensed its danger. The Communist Party would not let this movement pass lightly, for it meant a great loss of Party authority, and its challenge posed a threat to the Party's very existence. People also realized that whether this movement ended in victory or in failure, it would be a major historical event.

Some say that after Hu Yaobang died, the first to respond were not ordinary students, but students in the writing course at Beijing University. The first wreath laid in front of the Monument to the People's Heroes was also sent by young writers, editors, and reporters.

One of them, Zhang Boli, later became the main leader of the students in Tiananmen Square, and is now high on the Party's wanted list. Zhang Boli was born into a farmer's family in Heilongjiang Province, at China's northern tip—one of the country's poorest provinces. He is only too familiar with poverty and lack of power, with all the bureaucratic outrages the people of that fertile land have suffered. He became a reporter for a railway newspaper, and witnessed more of conservative local officials' ignorance and abuse of power. He is not only a reporter, but also a poet. People often think he is younger than he actually is—Zhang is in his thirties.

Zheng Yi, author of the novel *The Old Well,* which was later made into a movie, is ten years older than Zhang Boli. He was "reeducated" by the farmers in the countryside of Shanxi Province during the Cultural Revolution. He was one of the most representative among that generation of "educated youth." He had experienced the entire process of the Cultural Revolution at the lowest level and knew at first hand the damage the Communist Party had done to the people. And he refused to comply. Somewhere around the beginning of 1979, when he published a novella entitled *Maple,* he had already decided what he was going to do. That novella was the first to expose the social evils of the Cultural Revolution; it describes a pair of lovers who blindly follow Mao Zedong, join two different factions, and later become enemies.

In recent years, Zheng Yi has been writing a long novel set in Guangxi Province, where the Cultural Revolution was the most savage, and where the most people were killed. As soon as the student movement started in Beijing, he plunged right in. He lived and ate with the students, demonstrated with them, and gave them some brotherly advice. He hates injustice. He poured his hatred for the evil forces in China through the past twenty years into the struggle against Deng and his clique. During the forty days or more of demonstrations, he brought his young wife to participate in all the activities, and never left

Tiananmen Square. People say that he has been arrested, and all who know him are worried. For if he fell into the hands of the conservatives, they would not let him off easily. China would lose one of its brightest stars of literature, for Zheng has both the talent and the passion to be a great writer.

Some people came to the movement by other routes. The young scholar Liu Xiaobo was not very interested in politics; in fact, he despised and hated politics. After Hu Yaobang died, Liu published an article in the *China News Daily,* a Chinese-language New York newspaper, in which he said he did not think much of the student movement. His opinions were unusual: For instance, he thought Hu Yaobang was only the leader of the Party, and that we should not honor him so. Instead, we should honor Wei Jingsheng, who had been imprisoned by the Communist Party ten years earlier for fighting in the Democracy movement. Nonetheless, Liu Xiaobo eventually decided to participate in the movement. At first he had intended to stay in the United States; he believed that he could influence the student movement from there. But two days prior to the massacre, he and three other intellectuals announced a fast in Tiananmen Square to protest the savage attitude the Party had displayed toward the students. Within two days he was arrested, interrogated, and tortured.

All the writers, scholars, and journalists who were involved in the movement participated in all its activities—demonstrations, blocking of military vehicles, and providing support for students in the square. Literary critics could be seen shouting in streets and alleys, calling people to block army vehicles; famous writers ran around in a sweat, buying urinals for students. Scholars of the Chinese Academy of Social Sciences were also very active. Groups of people from many research institutes came to join the movement. University professors plunged in, also abandoning their usual discreet and retiring behavior.

A major feature of this movement was that many intellectuals who used to be timid and apolitical got involved. Those who had been involved became even more so.

The political scientist Yan Jiaqi is one of the many intellectuals whose attitudes had changed in recent years as China's social crises intensified, and popular anger and frustration grew. This modest and amiable middle-aged scholar was in the government's good graces a few years ago, when he published such works as *Ten-Year History of the Cultural Revolution* and *On Heads of Governments* and became director of the Research Institute of Political Science. Since then, he has worked in the Research Institute for Reforming the Political System—Zhao Ziyang's brain trust. But during the 1987 anti-liberalization movement, he was blacklisted. In 1988 he held that in the future, China should adopt a federal system, which really offended Deng Xiaoping. Deng wanted to hold him responsible and penalize him for that remark. During this Democracy movement he at first demanded only democracy. But by the middle of May, he had grown so frustrated by the government that he suddenly advocated the slogan "Down with the autocrat!"—obviously aimed at Deng Xiaoping.

Like all Chinese, scholars of the Chinese Academy of Social Sciences were surprised to see such a spring in Beijing. In recent years, they had had some serious discussions in specialized fields. Some scholars had conducted detailed studies of how to reform China's economic and political system, and a few had even made concrete plans for reform. However, little had been done to provide a general understanding of Chinese society (especially at its lowest levels), and, based on that study, to choose a course of development and change for China. There was almost no attention paid to how the different forces struggled within the Communist Party, and specifically, how to treat the democratic forces within the Party. Thus the movement lacked guidance in theory and in strategy. It never rose from being a spontaneous reaction, to become a self-determined force. Intellectuals should have played a bigger part in that respect. We should not have expected them to play the same role as the students.

Chinese scholars were all very busy. They had endless papers to write, articles they had promised newspapers and journals. There were endless seminars and symposiums to attend. They also had to meet foreign guests, and visitors from Hong Kong and Taiwan, as well as reporters. There were trips abroad to give lectures each year. They had very little time to make contact with people at the lowest level of society. They also did not know or understand contemporary Chinese students. Like most Chinese, they had not expected that a democracy movement of such a scale would take place.

Writers occupy a higher position in Chinese hearts than in Western countries. However, fewer and fewer Chinese writers think they should use their writing to help the Chinese people to reorganize society. One common view is that it would destroy the artistic purity of their work and cause it to lose the value of timelessness. Some writers were also growing indifferent to popular sentiments and to the country's fate. The Chinese people therefore turned to nonfiction writers and journalists, who lived up to their expectations.

27

Within a week in mid-May, almost all the major Beijing newspapers extricated themselves from forty years of control by the Party and became "liberal" newspapers. Only when you know the extreme attention the Chinese Communist Party pays to the control of ideology do you begin to appreciate how arduous this progress must have been, and how much courage it required.

The student movement reached its climax between May 14 and 20. One student leader said that without those few days of "liberal" newspapers, there would have been no such climax for the movement. The Communist Party would not admit that the student movement was patriotic and democratic—but the Party newspaper admitted it. It can be imagined how much encouragement the daily papers gave those who were fasting in Tiananmen Square. Young reporters, male and female alike, put their hearts inside Tiananmen Square. They did not come only to collect information; they were laughing and crying with the students. They shared everything with them—even the risk of being killed.

THE NEW IMAGE OF CHINA

The government refused to accept the most basic of students' demands: it refused to conduct a dialogue with students. Nor would it change its "counterrevolutionary rebellion" label for the movement. This infuriated both the students and the people of Beijing—for it meant that the ultimate judgment on the Democracy movement was totally negative, and unless that was changed, there was no hope for any improvement in the situation. Students had used all the methods available to them—demonstrations, sit-ins, slogans, and handing in written appeals. But Zhongnanhai remained implacable. The only way left was to fight to the death.

This created a tremendous contradiction: The cruel, despicable government was not good enough to be the students' opponent, much less worth their lives. Yet all the power and several million troops were in the hands of the government. The students therefore had to treat it as their opponent, and hope it might change its attitude. And students had to use nonviolent means.

At ten-thirty on May 13, in front of a building of Beijing University, about two hundred students gathered. They read the Pledge of Fasting issued under the name of the Fasting Committee of Beijing University. It read: "I pledge that in order to speed up the process of democratization of our country, for the prosperity of our motherland, I am willing to fast. I will resolutely abide by the disciplines of fasting, and will not cease until we reach our goals."

At noon, when the group arrived at Beijing Normal University, the number of those fasting increased to more than eight hundred. The twenty-one-year-old Wuer Kaixi, chairman of the Interim Student Association, led the group toward Tiananmen Square. By four in the afternoon, more than two thousand students who were fasting to appeal to the government had arrived. They were wearing white headbands with "FASTING" or "GIVE ME FREEDOM OR GIVE ME DEATH" written on them. At about five in the afternoon, a black flag rose on the flagpole in front of the Monument of the People's Heroes. On it was written "FASTING." At five-twenty, students read the Fasting Pledge aloud together under the monument, officially starting the fast.

29

The students thought that if they persisted in fasting for at most five days, the government would certainly make some concession under the pressure of public opinion. All the students had was the clothes they wore. They had nothing to cover themselves with. During the day, the temperature in the square was in the nineties. At night, it was chilly, especially sitting on the cold cement.

From that day, the people of Beijing gave their hearts to those in the square. Almost as soon as the fast began, volunteer teams of nurses, together with doctors and nurses from the Medical Institute, Peace Hospital, and Tongren Hospital came to provide medical aid. From then on, they were in the square with the students every day. At midnight, an old man using a small pushcart brought water to the students, saying in tears, "Anyway, you have to drink some water!"

At night, chilly winds blew across Tiananmen Square. People came on tricycles and in minibuses, bringing comforters, overcoats, and blankets from their own homes and tenderly covered the students.

What the students had not expected was that they could not soften the hearts of the Gang of the Old. They had no unreasonable demands. To show their sincerity, the students reduced their demands to two: First, recant the April 26 editorial in the *People's Daily* and recognize the student movement as patriotic; second, conduct an equal dialogue as soon as possible.

They selected representatives to staff a headquarters, led by Chai Ling, a graduate student from Beijing Normal University, her husband Feng Congde, and Li Lu, a student from Nanjing University, as commander-in-chief and vice-commanders. Members of the staff had clearly defined responsibilities. From then on, Tiananmen Square became highly organized, and all important decisions had to be made demo-cratically.

The student guard lines were preserving the safety of the students inside the square. Those who did not have a student ID were denied entry, without exception. They also formed a "lifeline" at the east side of the square in front of the Museum of Chinese History, to make a way for ambulances to pass through. People on the guard lines were not fasting, but they had to work around the clock. So people fainted from time to time, and ambulances carried them away. Those in the headquarters had to work while fasting.

By the third day of fasting, ambulances ran more frequently. During the first and second days, students still experienced stomach pains, but by the third day, they felt numb and dizzy, and their bodies felt like they were floating. They needed to lie still to rest, but the whole square was cluttered with garbage, the air stank, and the shouting of slogans was deafening. Many important people constantly came to visit them, so they had to shake hands and talk. Li Lu, one of the commanders, who had fainted several times in front of visitors, sat there thinking, "You are not doing us a favor by coming to visit us."

The government showed no sign of conceding. Chai Ling and Li Lu could tolerate this no longer. They thought of setting themselves afire simultaneously on May 15. In fact, every person who participated in fasting later was worried that the early fasters ran the risk of death. They all felt the same: Why should you die for us? Let us all die together! Student leaders and others felt responsible for the lives of the other students. Seeing the lives of three thousand students in danger, they naturally thought about sacrificing themselves. They even prepared the gasoline.

On May 16, headquarters was told that twelve students from the Central Drama Institute had announced that if they did not receive a clear answer from the government by three in the afternoon, they would also stop taking water. They were keeping their promise, lying inside the square. It was suicide to stop drinking at this time. The leaders tried to persuade them to drink. But they would not yield. Li Lu knelt beside the twelve students, not knowing what to say, weeping. He knew it would be of little use to say anything, but he still had to try: "Please let us die first, for we are the leaders! The only reason why I wanted to become the commander was to have a chance to die before others. But we cannot die in vain!"

At this moment, the leaders heard that students from Nankai University had also stopped drinking water. They taped their mouths shut to show their determination, and put a towel on top. Li Lu again knelt before them, begging them not to stop drinking. Eventually they took off the towels and plaster.

On May 16, six hundred students were taken to the hospital; on May 17, more than a thousand were taken. Every minute another ambulance sped through the crowds across Changan Avenue. Every siren tugged at people's hearts. Almost all the students who were taken to the hospital came back to the square; Chai Ling and Li Lu had come back three times. One of the student leaders, Wang Dan, returned to the square four times, saying: "I have to seek out Li Peng. If I have to die, I will die with him!"

The fasting brought popular anger toward the government to a head. The first to move were teachers. On May 15, the professors and staff of Beijing University carried a huge banner on their way to the square: "The students love us; and we love the students. Students are fasting, and our hearts ache. The government is coldhearted, and takes no notice. The lives of three thousand students are hanging on a string. We call on the whole world to protest against the government, and demand that it return us our students, return our human rights!"

More than half a million intellectuals from the Chinese Academy of Social Sciences, the Ministry of Culture, the Writers' Association, various newspapers, Xinhua News Agency, television stations, and various universities participated in the demonstration. One foreign reporter estimated that all the government ministries but one had members joining this demonstration. More than a million city residents cheered, with tears in their eyes. From May 16 on, people from all walks of life were mobilized. Every day, over a million people, through their demonstrations, supported the students' fast, and accused the government of being heartless. As of May 17, the number of people demonstrating reached three million. It would not be an exaggeration to say that every household in Beijing was out in the street in support of the students.

Reporters and editors of the *People's Daily* carried a banner which read, "RESOLUTELY OPPOSE THE APRIL 26 EDITORIAL!" Journalists from Xinhua News supported them, and entered the square at three in the afternoon. The Central People's Broadcasting Station reporters carried a sign saying, "CPBS NEWS: STUDENTS HAVE FASTED FOR THREE DAYS, FROM MAY 13 TO 15." Staff of the National Workers Union and workers of the Capital Iron and Steel Company shouted, "Workers are firm supporters of the students!" as they entered the square. There were slogans like "The Rule of the Gang of the Old Must Stop!" and "If the Premier Does Not Care, He Should Not Be Premier." People from Shaanxi, Guizhou, and

Guangxi carried a sign saying, "SECONDARY SCHOOL TEACHERS OF ELEVEN PROVINCES AND CITIES" and shouted slogans like "Supporting the Students."

By now, Tiananmen Square was packed. Changan Avenue was crowded with marchers in both directions. The Beijing Municipal Committee took away all the traffic police, so that there was no one to control the traffic. But it did not matter. Students controlled the traffic. And millions of citizens showed an amazing sense of discipline and self-control. During those days, there was no theft, no fighting, no traffic accident. There was perfect order.

Who were these young men and women in their twenties who were controlling the center of the capital? Compared with those who had engaged in the Democracy Wall protests in 1978 and 1979, these young people had not experienced so much suffering, had not thought about politics as much, and did not have as clear an idea of sacrificing themselves for the country. They did not even approve of a nation or a community demanding that its members sacrifice themselves for the general welfare. They were the most selfish generation since 1949. They were cynical, contemptuous of all authority, had no hope of nor good feeling toward the Communist Party. They did not think China had a future; nor did they think they had a responsibility for their country and society.

However, precisely because they valued their own feelings and individuality so highly, they could, compared with previous generations, least tolerate the suppression of individuality, the limits on freedom, and anything else against human nature that was imposed by the tradition created by the Communist Party. They grew up at a time when all traditions had lost their effect, so they never gave themselves up to the constraint of any party or ideology. Unlike the young people of the 1950s and 1960s, the students did not feel the need to be loyal to anything, or to sacrifice themselves for some commonly accepted goals. But when they did make a free choice, they were willing to sacrifice anything. One person the whole world remembers—Wang Weilin, who stood in front of a whole line of tanks—was one of them.

Those who had a relatively strong political sense among these young people, such as Wang Dan, Shen Tong of Beijing University, and Li Lu of Nanjing University, had for a long time been preparing for China's democratization. They had organized various societies and groups, seminars and discussions. In this way, they spread ideas of freedom among students. More student leaders were created during the movement, winning recognition by their courage, ability, and personal charm. These included Wuer Kaixi, Chai Ling, and many others. People were surprised to find that these few student leaders had such extraordinary ability at organization—they were able to organize the activities of several hundred thousand people so well that the opposition to the movement could find no excuse or pretext to use violence. They gave people sufficient reasons for their actions, imbued them with passion, and yet saw that they acted prudently.

THE EARTHQUAKE IN THE CORE: MISSING THE PERFECT OPPORTUNITY?

The movement, which had lasted for a month, was just reaching a climax. The struggle between the two forces within the Party had been going on since the start of the student movement, and now it reached the boiling point. A showdown was imminent. Of course, everything was still kept secret. However, unlike other struggles, this time it was hard to cover everything up completely. Several times, the conflict between Zhao Ziyang, Deng Xiaoping, and Li Peng was nearly exposed in front of everyone in China.

Two years before, the fall of Hu Yaobang as general secretary of the Party had been sudden, and it shook China deeply. Zhao Ziyang had played an important part in ousting Hu Yaobang, but after only two years as general secretary, Zhao was already finding that his position was not very stable. The Gang of the Old in the Central Committee wanted to blame the unprecedented inflation and growing economic crisis of 1988 on Zhao.

In February and March of 1989, Li Xiannian of the Gang of the Old suddenly became active. He openly expressed his discontent with Deng's decision to keep Zhao in his leadership role. Later, it was said that other members of the Gang of the Old helped persuade Deng to oust Zhao. Deng had already agreed to strip Zhao of his position as general secretary. During the next conference of the Military Commission, Deng now planned to strip Zhao of his position as first vice-chairman of the commission.

Zhao Ziyang resisted. The burgeoning student movement in Beijing and throughout the country gave him the chance to improve his position. He could not let it pass.

On Zhao's return from Korea on April 29, Li Peng met him at the airport and said, "The students are very dissatisfied with you." He then related what the student representative had said to Yuan Mu about a certain leader playing golf every week, and that people said Zhao's eldest son Zhao Dajun engaged in illegal trade. Zhao at once wrote a letter to the Standing Committee of the Politburo, saying that, according to customary law, if there is no one to make accusations, there can be no prosecution for economic crime. "But an exception can be made for my son. In the past, I intentionally did not let my son be an official, in order to avoid charges of a illicit influence. But I had not expected that he would have such problems doing trade. I now propose to the Central Disciplinary Committee to open an investigation of my son's economic problems, and treat him according to law. I hope that you publicize it throughout the country." Seeing this, Li Peng asked Zhao: "By doing this, are you not trying to put pressure on the Old Ones?"

In Party meetings, Zhao had said several times that he did not believe the student movement was manipulated by a few conspirators. Rather, they acted out of love for the country and the hope of accelerating the pace of reform. He also told Li Peng that the students wanted the government to admit that the April 26 editorial was mistaken. But since the editorial had been written to fit to Deng's ideas, recanting would be awkward. He offered to take full responsibility for having written the editorial, and to accept the demands of the students, and stop calling the movement a "counterrevolutionary rebellion." Li Peng did not agree. So Zhao made his ideas public.

On May 4, at a meeting of the board of the Asian Development Bank, Zhao Ziyang said, "The basic slogans for the student movement are 'support the Communist Party,' 'support socialism,' 'support the constitution,' 'speed up reform and democracy,' and 'oppose corruption.' They demand that we correct our mistakes and improve our work. To recognize our achievements and correct our mistakes is exactly what our Party advocates." He thought the student demands were reasonable; reform should be rational and orderly: "What is needed most of all right now is to keep calm, rational. Use restraint and order to solve problems through democracy and law."

This became one of the "crimes" of Zhao Ziyang. Twenty days later, Yang Shangkun, president of the country and vice-chairman of the Standing Committee of the Military Commission, accused Zhao at an urgent enlarged meeting of the Military Commission:

> Why is the capital out of control? Why are there demonstrations throughout the country? Students are the ones that are demonstrating, but the root is within the Party. That is to say, there are two voices within the Politburo. Two different voices. In Li Xiannian's words, there are two headquarters. The clearest example is the speech made at the meeting of the board of directors of the Asian Development Bank. It is understandable to say that the student movement is patriotic. But later it was said that we also had problems of corruption, agreeing with the students, and that we would solve these problems through democracy and law. This way of speaking avoided the fundamental issue of whether the April 26 editorial was correct or not. It thus exposed the difference of opinion inside the Standing Committee of the Central Committee to the students, making them more determined. That is why there are slogans like "Support Zhao Ziyang!" and "Down with Deng Xiaoping!" and "Down with Li Peng!"

At the enlarged meeting of the Standing Committee of the Politburo, Zhao Ziyang presented a six-point plan. He felt that if the Party accepted it, the actions would reduce student discontent, for their demands agreed with the Party's goals. First, investigate all the major companies run by children of high-ranking officials, and publicize the results of such investigations. Second, publicize the experience and accomplishments that qualified the officials for their important positions. Third, cancel special supplies for officials below the level of vice-minister and under the age of seventy-five. Fourth, the People's Congress should establish a supervisory committee to consider accusations of criminal activities by the children of high-ranking officials. Fifth, expand the freedom of the press as soon as possible. Sixth, make the judicature independent, and let all problems be solved in accordance with legal procedures.

Wan Li, head of the Standing Committee of the People's Congress, agreed with Zhao's proposal. Li Peng said that it was only Zhao's personal opinion, and therefore it could not be distributed to the lower levels as a resolution. Wan Li nevertheless distributed the proposal to the vice-chairmen and Party members of the People's Congress. When Li Peng heard of this, he tried to stop Wan Li. Wan, furious, asked Li Peng: "Who is in charge of whom? The government or the People's Congress?"

The reason Li Peng so boldly blocked Zhao was because Deng and the Gang of the Old were on his side. Zhao, on the other hand, had only an empty title as general secretary of the Party.

What actually happened at the upper levels of the Communist Party between May 10 and May 20 may be learned by future historians. But whatever happened, the struggle must have been intense. At least until May 17, certainly, Zhao had not given up.

In the afternoon of May 16, Zhao Ziyang met with Mikhail Gorbachev, general secretary of the Communist Party of the Soviet Union. Zhao said that the first plenary session of the Thirteenth Central Committee had made an important decision in 1987—that on major issues the Politburo would let Deng Xiaoping make the final decision, even though at his own request, Deng had already left the Central Committee and the Standing Committee of the Politburo. The whole country was watching the conversation live on TV. It was no secret that Deng had the supreme power inside the Party. But to legalize it in a secret meeting of a plenary session of the Central Committee was too much. People found Deng's hypocrisy in the charade of giving up power, and the other leaders' compliance with it, deplorable.

What amazed them even more was that Zhao dared to mention the fact publicly to Gorbachev. Why did he reveal this Party secret now? Had he sensed that he had no power to deal with the student movement, and thought that by saying this he would be forgiven by the people? Or was it because he wanted to attribute all the confusion to Deng Xiaoping, get the support of public opinion, and by so doing escape Deng's tyranny? Most people believed the latter.

Meanwhile, Deng and members of the Gang of the Old were reaching a secret a decision that would soon be made official. Around May 20, they would label Zhao as the head of the anti-Party clique, whose members included Hu Qili (member of the Standing Committee of the Politburo), Qin Jiwei (minister of National Defense), and Tian Jiyun (vice-premier of the State Council). The fifth one being discussed was Hong Xuezhi (former head of the General Logistics Department of the Military Commission). From this picture, it is clear that Zhao had the support of at least two high military officials who had substantial power.

By this time, seven high-ranking military officers had already expressed disagreement with the idea of suppressing the student movement with force. Sources say that if the letter of appeal by military officials had been circulated a few days more before being made public, it would have gained the signature of more than a hundred officials. Of the eight military divisions, at least three were very reluctant in their support of martial law and suppression of the students. The fast in Tiananmen Square had already aroused unprecedented sympathy and support from people all over China and from some officials in the Central Committee. All the mass media in the capital sided with the students. Even within some key departments, within the Office of the Central Committee, and within the garrison of the Central Committee there were conflicts, with a considerable number of officials and soldiers on the side of the students.

Many people hoped Zhao Ziyang would make a speech on TV to tell the people what had actually happened since April, and to give his opinion on how to deal with the present crisis. If he did this, the center of power might shift to his side. The Democracy movement might have won a complete victory.

But Zhao did not do this. His own personality and experience may have played a part at this historic moment. Since his youth, Zhao had lived within the circle of the Communist Party bureaucracy. Through the cruel struggles within the Party, he had learned to protect himself by discretion, by following all the rules, and by not giving others excuses to

41

accuse him. Like a lot of other leaders, he had an excess of steadiness but a deficit of boldness and courage. Hesitant to take action, he missed a golden opportunity.

NATIONAL SHAME ON MAY 19

The unforgettable May 19: At four-fifty in the morning, Zhao Ziyang came to Tiananmen Square to visit the fasting students. He urged them to stop the fast, saying, "We have come too late." These words expressed his frustration. Since the beginning of the student movement, Zhao had been seeking permission to visit the students. But Li Peng and Yang Shangkun had accused Zhao of "splitting the Party," which limited his freedom to act. Zhao continued, "You are still young. It was not easy for your parents and the country to bring you up. You should treasure your health. I am old. It doesn't matter too much. . . ." So saying, he burst into tears.

Listening to Zhao's words and looking at his graying hair, people sensed that he had lost most of his power. As he said to Gorbachev, power was in the hands of Deng Xiaoping. In the power struggle within the Party, Zhao was in the minority. As to whether to negate the April 26 editorial and reevaluate this movement as a patriotic movement, he said only that there were complicated problems, and that he believed there would be correct conclusions in the future. This was the clearest possible hint of his true feelings.

Many people were worried that this would be Zhao Ziyang's farewell speech. Li Peng accompanied Zhao, somber and silent, watching Zhao Ziyang.

After Zhao left the square, student leaders discussed the situation with the demonstrators and conducted heated debates.

Meanwhile, several mysterious figures in military uniform appeared in the square. They sought out the student leaders and reminded them that troops would soon enter the square. They must get ready to remove the wounded and the sick, or the consequences would be unimaginable.

At nine that night, the eighth day of fasting, the "Voice of the Student Movement," the temporary radio station broadcasting from the square, announced that the fast was over and the sit-in had begun.

This was the night when ambulances were the busiest.

The three thousand fasters were on the brink of collapse. In every sense, there was not much time left. Medical personnel, drivers, students, and civilians were extremely busy. The lifeline already extended from the Museum of Chinese History to both sides of Changan Avenue. Guard lines were vigilant. Within minutes of hearing the ambulance sirens, the lifeline would be opened. Almost a hundred ambulances rushed by. People cried, "Save the children! Save China!"

At ten in the evening, the procession from Zhongnanhai began. High-ranking officials of the Central Committee, the Party, and the military did not dare use their imported cars; they used Chinese-made cars instead. They were hurrying to the auditorium of the General Logistics Department in the southwest section of Beijing.

Li Peng announced to the assembled officials that Beijing was witnessing a serious rebellion that must be stopped. Then Yang Shangkun made a speech. He said that troops called in from other parts of China were entering Beijing, and would establish martial law. Teeth clenched, waving his hands in the air, Li Peng obviously thought victory was certain.

Shortly before midnight, official loudspeakers were announcing the meeting and speeches made by Li Peng and Yang Shangkun. The news was broadcast six times every hour. Every time it was broadcast, students shouted, "Down with Li Peng!" "Oppose martial law!" These waves of shouting rose from the hearts of thousands of people. How could the denizens of Zhongnanhai stop them?

The editors and reporters in the official propaganda machinery once again supported the people. They were shouting to each other, "Let's go to Tiananmen Square!" "Let's protect the students!" More and more people gathered in the square. Students, workers, and residents once again organized lines to surround the square and extend to Changan Avenue. These lines, made of flesh and blood, would be fighting to the death with bullets made of steel. Within the square, the students were reducing their area for better defense. People from many universities were entering the square to support them. Residents stood with the students and guarded various major entries to the square. They showed no signs of fear.

At the Hujialou intersection, several miles to the northeast, people were irritated by Li Peng's speech. They began to go out to the streets, and some young people started for Tiananmen Square on their bicycles.

"Is this true?" people were asking.

A canvas-covered truck was approaching. It was not a bus, or a cargo truck. If you took a closer look, you could see that it was full of soldiers. Three old ladies lay down on the street and shouted, "Run over me!"

The truck squealed to a stop. The soldiers were astonished. They were under orders to suppress the counterrevolutionary rebellion; they thought they would be welcomed by the people, and they never expected this reaction.

An engineer of a certain research institute had been an "expert" all his life, and was not interested in politics. To use his own words, he was using silence to protect his conscience. He was silent and sighing at the beginning of the student movement. But when he saw Yuan Mu with the students on TV, he shouted angrily, pointing at Yuan Mu, "Are you a fucking human being?" It was the first time he had cursed in his entire fifty-eight years. After that outburst he became silent again, and went to work as usual. He also ate dinner as usual, and asked his two sons to finish eating quickly. Then they went downstairs, carried bricks, stones, and cement blocks for barricades and pushed buses over to block traffic. Then he sat down by the roadside and smoked.

It was like this every day for two weeks.

In a province, a noted poet had already passed the age of sixty. After hearing martial law announced by Li Peng, he came all the way to Tiananmen Square and stood by the Golden River Bridges in front of Tianan Gate, weeping. He said that he wanted to embrace all the children and give his heart to them, that he wanted to write a poem with only one sentence—"I see China's hope!" At night, he slept with the students. One of them gave him two old newspapers to lay on the ground, and a brick as a pillow. He said he was so glad to be able to spend the night with the students. He also hoped there would be a tank coming over, so that he could fight it with his body. "Aside from this bunch of old bones," he said, "I have only my conscience."

On the second day, the students respectfully calling him teacher, sent him out of the square with tears. He stayed in a friend's house, right at an intersection where the army trucks passed. So every night he came out to block the trucks, then smoked a cigarette, his mind at ease.

In an epoch-making act, all the people came out to block the army vehicles. The 300,000 soldiers were blocked by the people with their bodies and their sense of justice.

An old man at Shijingshan said to the soldiers: "Forty years ago, we welcomed the soldiers of the People's Liberation Army; now forty years later, you come here to suppress the students, and this we will not allow!"

Beginning on May 15 and ending on May 19, there were five days of freedom of the press. The press provided objective reporting of the Democracy movement. Students and citizens invited the soldiers to read the papers. But the soldiers said they were not allowed to read the newspapers, watch the news on TV, or listen to the radio. All they knew was that they were going to perform a military task to safeguard the Party Central Committee. They had no idea of what was happening in Beijing. When the people told them what had been happening in Tiananmen Square, even the soldiers cried.

Everyone blocked military vehicles; even thieves took part. On May 24, there was an announcement at Xidan Market saying that thieves would go on strike for ten days and concentrate on blocking military vehicles.

The intersection of Sanhuan Road and Tuanjiehu in the northeast part of the city was another major point for blocking military vehicles. About a dozen young people who admitted that they were thieves worked hard to set up roadblocks. At night, they told the residents to rest, saying they would shout if there was anything new. An old man said, "Good. Go on like this. Learn from the college students. Don't be ashamed to correct your past mistakes." "Rest easy," the thieves replied. "If we ever steal again, it will be in Li Peng's house!" They won loud applause.

More than three hundred motorcycles belonging to Beijing's private entrepreneurs were used to form a "flying-tiger team." They ran along Changan Avenue to pass information about the troops to the student headquarters. Whenever and wherever they went, they were greeted with warm applause and cheers. Pedicab drivers also formed a group to rescue the wounded.

Five helicopters hovered above Tiananmen Square. Then there were three. It was said that they had just been brought in to deal with students and citizens. In order to distract the helicopters, kites were flown and balloons were sent into the sky. Students of the Aviation Institute also made simple model airplanes. All flew into the sky, so that the helicopters did not dare come down. They dropped leaflets and went away.

Some of the leaflets fell on the Great Hall of the People. Some fell into Zhongnanhai. And some packs never opened and dropped right on the roof of the Chairman Mao Memorial Hall with a big thump, frightening the workers inside the hall. It was discovered later that this package, which should have contained Li Peng's speech, instead held dozens of copies of an announcement and the open letter by the seven sympathetic generals. Li Peng and his troops were very upset, claiming that they would look into this "major case."

All the efforts of the government were in vain. Demonstrations took place in Shanghai, Guangzhou, Shenzhen, and Chongqing. Even with a warning of a Force 8 hurricane, people in Hong Kong and Macao came out into the streets in the pouring rain and shouted, "Down with Li Peng!" "Oppose martial law!" Troops in Beijing began to retreat.

At the end of May, demonstrations supporting martial law, organized and approved by the Municipal Committee in Beijing, appeared in the suburbs of the city. Farmers shouted, "Down with Fang Lizhi!" Some reporters asked them, "Who is Fang Lizhi?" The answer came promptly: "I don't know. I am paid to shout." It turned out that every demonstrator had been given 10 yuan and one straw hat for going into the street and shouting.

THOUGHTS AT THE SCENE

Toward the end of May, the Democracy movement in Beijing was ebbing. The students were exhausted. Nobody could see how the problems could be solved. The number of people in Tiananmen Square dwindled.

But this did not affect the optimism of the people in Beijing. From the middle of April, Beijing had been enveloped in a special atmosphere. After martial law was declared, many Chinese who were abroad were worried. They called Beijing. What they heard was laughter. Someone let the other side listen through the receiver: "Listen, this is the sound of helicopters!" "This is the sound of people shouting in Tiananmen Square."

They had reason to be optimistic: Hundreds of thousands of soldiers had been stopped outside Beijing by ordinary people. Martial law was totally ineffective. How could Li Peng go on being premier? People guessed that Deng Xiaoping would surely get rid of Li Peng—and that this would take place within a few days. But what happened was the reverse: Deng got rid of Zhao Ziyang.

This did not create too much of a stir among the students. Students did not place too much hope in Zhao Ziyang. They did not like Zhao, nor did they want to associate their movement with Zhao's power struggle within the Party.

Is it possible that if the students had stopped the fast it would have been helpful to Zhao Ziyang and strengthened his position in his struggle with Deng Xiaoping and Li Peng? Perhaps. But that was not what the student leaders wanted to do. They did not want the student movement to have anything to do with the struggles within the Party.

But was the struggle between Zhao on the one hand and Deng and Li on the other only a power struggle? If so, then the struggle between Hu Yaobang and Deng Xiaoping should also be called a power struggle. But their commemoration of Hu Yaobang a month ago had not been insincere. In May 1989, Zhao Ziyang at least objectively represented the democratic forces of the Chinese people and the Party, even though only partially and only temporarily.

As a matter of fact, even among the students, most people did not approve of continuing the fast. On May 14, Wuer Kaixi and Shen Tong went to talk with the representatives of the Department of the United Front,* and its director, Yan Mingfu. He told them "If you must divide the Central Committee into factions, then your action is not helpful to the pro-reform faction. Zhao Ziyang's intentions would be very

---

*The United Front is the alliance of all parties united against the common enemy; this department of the Central Committee is in charge of liaison with non-Party intellectuals and overseas Chinese.

hard to realize." The student leaders were ready to end the fast, as long as the other side admitted that the movement was not a "counterrevolutionary rebellion." They would advise students to return to their schools and to continue to struggle to build a democratic way of life. But unfortunately the negotiation failed. The more than thirty student representatives all wept, feeling that they had not performed their task well.

However, since Gorbachev was in Beijing, and in order not to let the government lose face, they decided to move the students in the square to the east side, leaving a space in front of the Great Hall of the People for the welcoming ceremony. They also said that this was the first concession, and the last. Even so, they were not understood by the other students, and were called traitors.

There was an interesting interlude on May 14. Dai Qing, a woman writer, and eleven famous intellectuals came to Tiananmen Square. Dai Qing spoke to the students and asked them to stop fasting. But the students sensed that she was treating them as children and paid no attention to her. They hated to be called "kids." Her advice was rejected also because it advocated concession and compromise. Revolution could only go forward. Struggle could only be carried to the end. When Dai Qing advised them to stop fasting and to "take into consideration the overall situation," they thought, "What kind of 'overall situation'? It must be the 'overall situation of the government.' "

In the afternoon of May 16, Yan Mingfu, director of the Department of the United Front, came to Tiananmen Square on his own behalf, and spoke with tears over the loudspeaker: "Your actions, your spirit, have already touched all the Chinese people, have won their hearts and the hearts of the Party.

50

Please, for the motherland, for the sake of speeding up reform and democracy, you must treasure your health." He beseeched the students to give the leaders of the Central Committee more time and a chance to consider the matter. He also said that he was empowered to announce that there would be no revenge of any form against those who had participated in the demonstrations. He even said that if they did not believe him, he would be willing to stay in Tiananmen Square as hostage and sit with the students to prove he was sincere. Yan Mingfu was no ordinary Party official. He had always been sympathetic to students and intellectuals. But the students would not compromise—and those who urged them to do so were subject to strong criticism.

Wuer Kaixi had already had a similar experience. Once he had proposed that students should retreat from Tiananmen Square, and for that he was dismissed as chairman of the Students Association. In general, whoever was tough, resolute, and ruthless in strategy would gain popularity. Conversely, whoever was careful, flexible, took into consideration practical conditions, and proposed concession and compromise, would be despised and accused as a traitor.

The fast that started on May 13 and was carried to the extent of refusing liquids was dominated by the kind of radical attitude affected by those who fought regardless of their own lives. However, questions arose: If the government refused to accept the demands, should the fast continue indefinitely? Was this government worth the lives of several thousand students? Were fasting and death their goals? On the seventh day of the fast, May 19, thousands of students fell. It was hard to persuade them to stop fasting. Any decision had to be voted by a majority of the students. But the people in the square, who had already suffered so much pain, were unwilling to stop fasting and compromise.

After May 22, Zhao Ziyang had lost power. Now people focused on the National People's Congress. Originally, the National People's Congress had been nothing more than a rubber stamp in the hands of the Communist Party leaders, and could not function as it was supposed to according to law. However, in the past two years, people had strengthened their feeling for law and order. They hoped that at this important juncture, the National People's Congress could exercise the powers designated to it by law.

They all thought about visiting Wan Li, who was then chairman of the National People's Congress. Wan Li was one of the main representatives of the prodemocracy group within the Party. In the late 1970s and early 1980s, he had advocated fixing farm output for each household, acting as a pioneer in agricultural reform. In terms of changing the political system and ideology, he was more radical than Zhao Ziyang and even Hu Yaobang. This time, when he was in Canada, he openly expressed his feeling that the student movement was a patriotic movement, and made no attempt to paper over the differences between him and Deng Xiaoping.

Among the intellectuals, college students, and politicians who were on the side of Zhao Ziyang, Wan Li could perform two very important functions: First, if he could end his visit to Canada ahead of schedule and return to China, he could organize an emergency meeting of the Standing Committee of the National People's Congress, followed by a meeting of the full People's Congress itself, in order to end martial law and oust Li Peng as premier. If he did not have the power to do this, he could stay abroad on the pretext of illness, organize a balancing force against the antireform forces inside China, and issue a declaration denouncing Li Peng and the whole gang for violating the constitution and opposing martial law and the suppression of the student movement.

On May 24, Wan Li received a telegram asking him to return to China earlier than originally planned. Yan Jiaqi and other intellectuals had decided to organize one million people to welcome Wan Li on his return and to call a meeting of the People's Congress. But, contrary to everyone's expectation, Wan Li was detained in Shanghai because he was "in poor health and had to receive medical care in Shanghai." Three days later, Wan Li published a written statement saying that martial law in Beijing was in accordance with the constitution, thus disappointing proreform people in China and abroad.

However, attempts to organize an emergency meeting of the People's Congress did not stop. Hu Jiwei, former director of the *People's Daily* who was forced to resign in 1983 during the campaign against spiritual contamination, asked the Social Research Institute of the Stone Corporation, the largest private enterprise in China, to contact members of the Standing Committee. By the end of May, there were already thirty-eight members who had agreed to initiate an emergency meeting of the Standing Committee of the National People's Congress. However, this number did not reach the legal majority.

After the June 4 massacre, among the intellectuals the Gang of the Old had ordered to be arrested was Cao Siyuan, director of the Social Research Institute of the Stone Corporation.

They accused him of having a hand in attempting to call the emergency meeting of the People's Congress. Hu Jiwei was also questioned by the followers of the Gang of the Old at the meetings of the National People's Congress. They "investigated" this incident as a "major conspiracy related to Zhao Ziyang."

It is clear from their reaction that after they discovered at the end of May that the constitution formulated thirty-five years ago could in fact be implemented, they were frightened out of their wits, fearing that if the Standing Committee could be convened, the Li Peng government would really lose its legitimacy.

A month later, an intellectual who had fought shoulder to shoulder with the students in Tiananmen Square and who later fled abroad said with regret, "During this tragic movement, there was no fighting tactic, no strategy. It seemed as though people were unaware of what Lenin and Mao Zedong had said about strategies of revolutionary struggle. If you constantly hear slogans saying 'through to the end,' how could you be willing to make any concessions and attempts at reconciliation?"

Admittedly, student leaders like Wang Dan and Shen Tong were always calm, had enough sense to use strategy, and were willing to cooperate with the proreform forces within the Party. But as the movement unfolded, their influence dwindled. The mood of students who had been infuriated by the government was very hard to control. The "Left" tendencies and the "complete success at one stroke" that had been so destructive in the history of the Communist Party were again evident here. Until the morning of June 4, even when most students were persuaded to leave Tiananmen Square, some still refused to retreat.

After it was certain that Zhao Ziyang was out, and Wan Li had expressed his agreement with Deng, more and more people worried that military suppression was inevitable. But they felt that the worst would be a repeat of 1976, when the government used clubs to disperse students, and not bullets. Most of the Beijing students agreed they should leave the square. But the majority of students in the square by this time came from other parts of China. On May 27, there was a resolution that there would be a citywide peaceful demonstration on May 30, and students would then leave the square. A difference of opinion arose, however, between the Beijing students and those from other parts of China. So the time of departure was postponed to June 20, when the Standing Committee of the National People's Congress was to open its meeting. But the next day, they decided that the date of departure would be indefinite—only after the government met the following demands: (1) lift martial law; (2) remove the troops; (3) guarantee that there would be no revenge afterward; and (4) provide freedom of the press.

The beauty and the ugliness of human nature made a striking contrast in the sunshine of Beijing's spring. The students' sincerity, bravery, and spirit of self-sacrifice moved the people of Beijing, as well as some of the officials.

On the other hand, the vile, the ugly, and the despicable in human nature were also exposed on the streets of Beijing and in Tiananmen Square. The people's government used all the means available to watch over and investigate its own people. There were often a few thousand plainclothes police working in Tiananmen Square. In Beijing hotels, on Changan Avenue, or in the square, countless undercover agents used disguises as well as video cameras to record people's activities. All the active members of the movement were followed. Officials secretly searched their residences, stole their means of transportation, and used all means available to threaten them. In Tiananmen Square, when several people wanted to drink from a bottle of water because they were thirsty, they suddenly noticed a strange smell coming from the bottle. It was actually sulfuric acid. At the height of the fast, when it was very hot, the government suddenly cut off the water supply to the square. It was only due to the intercession of the International Red Cross that water was restored. In late May, just when the army troops were going to use tear gas to disperse students and people in Beijing, the Beijing Department Store was ordered not to sell towels and gauze masks to anyone who looked like a student.

THE MASSACRE

The political situation in China became clear at the beginning of June. The government had finished its preparations for the bloody repression. Equipped with armored vehicles, tear gas, rubber bullets, tanks, and even the dumdum bullets that were internationally forbidden, over 300,000 soldiers were ready to slaughter the people. Deng Xiaoping had formed an alliance with the Gang of the Old. Now, they were ready to act.

On the morning of June 2, a vehicle full of armed police without a license plate was going at high speed until it got to Fuxingmenwai Street, where it hit a pedicab, killing two people instantly. Another person was wounded and sent to the hospital, but died before being treated. People surrounded the police vehicle and found uniforms and weapons.

On the morning of June 3, the Beijing Municipal Committee held what the newspapers called a "Mobilization Meeting before Going to the Front Line"—the title of an article of more than eight thousand words, "clarifying the nature of this rebellion and the necessity for martial law." Xinhua News Agency distributed this article nationwide, indicating that a major action was not far away.

Meanwhile, troop maneuvers started in an atmosphere of tension. Four tourist buses were seen heading toward Tiananmen Square from east and west at the same time. Inside sat young men wearing white shirts, looking like peasants sightseeing in Beijing. But vigilant residents stopped the buses and found that those inside were not young sightseers, but soldiers without uniform coats and caps. They also found machine guns, submachine guns, hand grenades, and clubs.

A preview of the massacre took place at noon on June 3. Three thousand soldiers and armed police with helmets and clubs rushed out of the west gate of Zhongnanhai and blocked Fuyou Street and the intersection of Liubukou Street. After they surrounded the civilians, they issued a warning. Ten minutes later, they threw twenty tear-gas bombs. While everyone was blinded by the gas, the soldiers wielded clubs, and old people and children began to fall to the ground. Meanwhile, more than three hundred soldiers rushed out of Xinhua Gate, wielding electric clubs, and beat everyone they saw. Students from the Institute of Politics and Law, who had been sitting in front of Xinhua Gate for two weeks, were taken by surprise. There was general disorder. At two in the afternoon, the western portal of the Great Hall of the People—on the side away from the square—suddenly opened to release more than ten thousand armed police, trying to link up with the soldiers and armed police in Xidan and Xinhuamen, and thus to separate the civilians into smaller groups that could be surrounded and controlled.

But more than three hundred thousand people confronted the troops, refusing to let them advance. From the Great Hall of the People to Xidan, soldiers and people were deadlocked. Gradually the soldiers who had attempted to separate the demonstrators were themselves separated and surrounded by the people. People wearing clothes of different colors surrounded soldiers wearing uniforms and steel helmets.

Some residents who had been beaten raised blood-drenched clothes for others to see, and told of the brutality of the soldiers and armed police. There was still a smell of tear gas. The citizens became enraged. Some of them overturned an army jeep, destroyed a traffic-control tower, and smashed the windows of two tourist buses that had been used to transport weapons and ammunition.

On the evening of June 3, the darkest night of the People's Republic was under way. After six, television and radio stations broadcast three emergency announcements from the city government and the troops. They warned the people of Beijing that the soldiers could no longer tolerate the situation and would take measures to wipe out resistance. The announcements asked residents not to come out into the streets, for their own safety. But how could the residents abandon the students? Taking wet towels with them in case of tear-gas attacks, many rushed to Tiananmen Square on their bicycles from all over the city. There were already more than ten thousand people in the square—and the atmosphere was charged. While the third announcement was being broadcast, the first shot had already been fired near Huangtingzi, in the western suburbs. Witnesses say that a person fell following the shot.

At nine in the evening, huge numbers of troops began to march on Tiananmen Square. Soldiers from the eastern suburbs started down Jianguomen Street, which runs into Changan Avenue. The Jianguomen district is densely populated, so many people took part in blocking the army vehicles.

But there was an emergency in the west: The Gongzhufen and Muxidi districts were not so densely populated, so there were few people to block the vehicles of the Twenty-Seventh Division. Residents and students hurried there to help, headed by a daredevil team of workers with clubs in hand, and student guard lines holding flags.

By now, from the Military Museum of the Chinese People's Revolution to Muxidi and Xidan, gunshots resounded and smoke filled the air. Blood was flowing and bodies were lying in the streets. Soldiers of the Twenty-Seventh Division used light machine guns and semiautomatic weapons to shoot people in the street and in buildings on either side. Workers and residents coming to help saw a long line of armored vehicles coming from the west at full speed, and hurriedly retreated to the Xidan district. They used everything they could find, from bricks to trucks, to build roadblocks. A worker set fire to the four buses and two trucks that were lying in the middle of the road, shouting, "The People's Liberation Army does not kill people!" and "Whoever suppresses the student movement will come to no good end!"

The armored vehicles stopped. Soldiers jumped out. Suddenly the shouting of slogans also stopped. For a few minutes there was dead silence. The people still hoped that the soldiers would use only tear gas or rubber bullets. But at one command, the soldiers raised their guns and fired one round at the residents and students, who fell to the ground. As soon as the gunshots stopped, other people rushed forward to rescue the wounded. The steps of a clinic near Xidan were already covered with blood.

But the struggles at the intersections did not stop. Armored vehicles ran over roadblocks, knocked over cars and buses. The unarmed people had only bricks. So stones and bricks fell on the armored vehicles like rain, but what could they do to the armored vehicles?

What they got back in return was bullets, a hail of bullets from machine guns and semiautomatics. People dispersed and ran for their lives. Soldiers ran after them, guns blazing. Even when residents ran into a courtyard or into the shrubbery, the soldiers would catch up with them and kill them.

The battle at the Xidan intersection continued for more than half an hour. How could residents prevent the war machines from advancing? Within this half-hour, more than forty people were wounded or killed at this intersection alone.

Meanwhile, a bloody battle was also taking place on Changan Avenue to the east of Tiananmen Square. Two armored vehicles roared up at full speed, regardless of roadblocks and walls formed by people. People had to run away to avoid being hit. One armored vehicle even ran into another one; at least ten soldiers were thrown out, and one died instantly. Another vehicle ran over four people. Angry bystanders used crowbars to open the lid of the armored vehicle and forced it to a stop.

They set fire to it, forcing the soldiers to come out. Then they beat them up. But students who still insisted on nonviolence pulled the soldiers from the hands of the residents and sent them to the hospital.

Troops were advancing on Tiananmen Square from east and west. Residents and students from other parts of the city, concerned about the thousands of demonstrators still in the square, walked toward it. Passing the Xinhua Gate of Zhongnanhai, they saw soldiers washing the pavement with water. The students from the Institute of Politics and Law who had been sitting there a few hours earlier were nowhere to be seen.

One female doctor in a white work uniform stood there, crying. Her ambulance crew had earlier rescued a whole truckload of wounded students. When they returned, the soldiers did not allow her to rescue students again. The soldiers actually used guns to force the Red Cross ambulance to leave the scene.

After one in the morning, about six hundred soldiers were marching toward the Great Hall of the People from the west, in formation, four or five in a row, firing random shots into the air. They arrived at the hall at one-forty. By two o'clock in the morning, soldiers of the People's Liberation Army had surrounded several thousand students and other civilians—the people—inside Tiananmen Square. The students retreated to the steps of the Monument to the People's Heroes. They all had their wills inside their pockets. They were singing the "Internationale," hand in hand, waiting to wake up ancient China with their blood.

At four, all the lights in Tiananmen Square were suddenly turned off. The "evacuation order" was again broadcast. Meanwhile, the noted rock singer and composer Hou Dejian and the young literary critic Liu Xiaobo were negotiating with the military to let the students retreat from the square peacefully.

At four-forty, just as the students were starting to retreat out of the square, a red signal flare ripped the night sky. Searchlights suddenly bathed the square. Students found that they were surrounded by armed soldiers wearing helmets. Some of them had already set up a line of more than a dozen machine guns, aimed at the students. Other soldiers rushed in among the students and beat them with electric cattle prods and rubber-covered steel clubs. They tore their way up the base of the Monument to the People's Heroes, and forced the students down, beating them until their heads were bleeding. As they reached the ground level, the machine guns opened fire.

By now the square was surrounded on three sides by armored vehicles or tanks, leaving only one exit.

The students began to retreat from Tiananmen Square, moving westward toward Xidan. A tank caught up with the students from behind. First it fired tear gas, then it ran over where people were most crowded. Witnesses say that at least thirteen students were crushed in one spot alone. Judging from the remnants of their clothes, people could tell that five of them were women.

As the sun rose on June 4, the morning clouds were red. The soldiers continued to fire until they reached the diplomatic area at Jianguomen. More than three thousand people were killed in Tiananmen Square and on the streets of Beijing.

After the killing, there were massive arrests nationwide. People who were involved in the Democracy movement were executed in Beijing, Shanghai, Chengdu, Changsha, Wuhan.

The Communist Party of China boasted that it had smashed a "counterrevolutionary rebellion."

From June 4 to the beginning of August, 120,000 people who were involved with the movement were thrown into prison. And 20,000 were imprisoned in Beijing alone. Secret arrests, interrogations, and torturings were conducted in the darkness. The maniacal Gang of the Old cried in delirium: "We must catch them all! Imprison them all! Kill them all! We must pluck out the weeds by the root!"

The world must not forget China, China in the spring of 1989. If executioners like Li Peng and the Gang of the Old are not punished, how can humanity have a moment of peace?

2

WHY IT HAPPENED

At the center of Tiananmen Square stands the Monument to the People's Heroes of the Chinese Revolution. Carved into it are scenes from the bloody, centuries-long struggle between a democratic China struggling to be born and an autocratic China that has so far refused to die. There are portrayals of the great peasant uprising in the Taiping revolution of the nineteenth century, and episodes showing the brutality of Western imperialism. And of course there are depictions of the heroic leadership of the Communist Party, which temporarily succeeded in shaping this deep-seated demand for China to free itself at last and build a more just society.

The bullet holes that pocked the monument in June were quickly hidden. But what the troops did that day will never be forgotten. At the center of Beijing, at the symbolic heart of the revolution, this government showed its complete bankruptcy. It still had the tanks; for now, they could still be turned upon peaceful protests for change. But the savagery unleashed by a discredited autocratic leadership brutally exposed the conflict between the old autocratic China and the struggle for a new democratic China. The very Party that had erected that monument to the heroes of revolution now stood for the old autocratic ways. And in forcing a new generation of heroes to arise, it had clung to one of the oldest feudal illusions of China—that autocracy is essential to guarantee stability.

It is an illusion deeply imbedded in Tiananmen's own history. For though "Tiananmen" in Chinese means "Gate of Heavenly Peace," the gate was designed by Yongle, one of the most brutal emperors in Chinese history. By building this highest of all the gates to imperial palaces in China, he sought both to show the highly concentrated power he held and to call upon heaven to grant him eternal and stable rule.

But the Ming dynasty was not stable. Conflict was continuous. And within two centuries after it was built, Li Zicheng led a peasant army into Beijing, shooting an arrow right through the character "heaven," so prominently displayed on the gate.

Not until the twentieth century was it possible to radically challenge that autocratic system. When the May Fourth movement swept over China in 1919 to protest China's shabby treatment at the Versailles Peace Conference, protesters demanded democracy and science. Four thousand students, led by those from Beijing University, gathered in Tiananmen to attack the treaty and call for a new China. They were but a symbol of the growing number of intellectuals and activists who throughout China called for freedom and human rights, as well as a more prosperous and modern society. The call came from across much of the political spectrum—from the well-known Communist Chen Duxiu to the liberal Hu Shi to the writer Lu Xun, who vehemently attacked China's "man-eating autocracy."

They called for a democratic China. What "democracy" meant to them was not entirely clear—except that it was passionately believed to embody the antithesis of autocratic rule. It was an affirmation of human dignity and personal freedom, but it was also a way of releasing the enormous talent and energy of the Chinese people. That could come only with the end of old autocratic ways.

The Chinese Communist Party, founded in 1921, tapped and shaped this deep demand for change among the Chinese people. It proclaimed itself the successor of the May Fourth period—and of the hopes of the Chinese people for a "New Democracy." In fighting to end the Japanese invasion and the autocratic ways of the Kuomintang, the Party won the support of vast numbers of the Chinese people. In 1949, when Mao Zedong proclaimed in Tiananmen Square, "The Chinese people have stood up!" many people felt that the distance between the top of the gate and the ground had become smaller. Here, at last, was a government that would not simply revert to the autocratic ways of old.

Of course, in retrospect the hope seems an illusion. The possibilities that did exist were crushed, and over the years, attacked with growing vehemence by Mao and others. Tiananmen Square, enlarged by the Communists to its present size and shape, became the scene of huge parades celebrating the Communist order. Each October 1, on National Day, an elaborate commemoration and celebration of Communist rule was staged. And then during the Cultural Revolution came the demonstrations of millions of Red Guards, streaming in from all over China to pay homage to a nearly deified Chairman Mao.

But as Mao lay dying in 1976, that deep demand for a more democratic China burst forth once again. Again, Tiananmen became a symbol of protest. During the Qing Ming Festival, when the Chinese honor their dead, people spontaneously poured into the square to bring commemorative wreaths to mourn Zhou Enlai, who had died the previous January—and to quietly protest the looming presence of the Gang of Four. It was the first spontaneous outburst since the founding of the People's Republic in 1949. But the wreaths were seized; the people were forcibly removed from the square, and then banned from showing such mourning. Mao, now in his last months, labeled the events "the counterrevolutionary incident at Tiananmen Square." Deng Xiaoping was blamed for the event and was purged from all his positions.

Five months after the 1976 Tiananmen incident, Mao was dead. His chosen successor, Hua Guofeng, arrested Mao's widow and her gang, but sought to legitimize his rule by building the huge Mao Zedong Memorial Hall in Tiananmen Square.

Hua was not to last long. Within three years, Deng Xiaoping came to power, by drawing on the strength of the "Democracy Wall" movement that sprang up around Tiananmen and in many Chinese cities in 1978 and 1979, and on a growing demand within the Communist Party itself for deep change. The connection between the two forces—popular expression

and Party reformers—was never a direct or easy relationship, but it is a central aspect of the story that follows. Without it Deng's reforms would never have attained what successes they did. But Deng, though he well knew how to appear the embodiment of the Chinese people's hopes for reform, was never at ease with its deeper democratic implications. For far too long, the Chinese people hoped that he would lead the way toward political as well as economic change; for too long, the emphasis was placed on the role of this single man. The last time Deng Xiaoping appeared in Tiananmen Square was October 1, 1984, the celebration of the thirty-fifth anniversary of the founding of the People's Republic. When the students saw him, they raised flags that said "How are you, Xiaoping!"

Today, that hope lies brutally murdered. When students went to Tiananmen Square this year to demand political reform, Deng ordered, "Arrest every one of them." And in the last parade before the massacre, the placards said, "How confused you are, Xiaoping!"

THE EMERGENCE OF REFORM

The movement toward democracy after Mao's death broke out amid conflict among the three Party factions that emerged after the Third Plenary Session of the Eleventh Central Committee in December 1978. One faction held that economic reform had to be combined with democratic change. Hu Yaobang represented those seeking to democratize politics and promote market reforms. Another faction advocated a combination of autocratic political rule and a free economy, what Tariq Ali calls "Market Stalinism." Zhao Ziyang represented this group. A third faction advocated all-out Stalinism in both politics and economics. Reform for them meant only "market adjustment"—a "birdcage economy." Its spokesman was Chen Yun. Perched uneasily over these factions and competing visions was Deng Xiaoping. In many ways he became the ultimate arbitrator among them, and his story is thus inseparable from the fate of China's reform effort.

In October 1976, Hua Guofeng, Ye Jianying, and Wang Dongxing joined together to arrest the Gang of Four, which included Mao's widow. They did not plan to correct Mao's mistakes. They continued to speak of Mao's theory of "continuing the revolution under the dictatorship of the proletariat" and proposed two "as-long-ases": "As long as the policy was suggested by Mao, we will support it; as long as it is Mao's directive, we will inexorably follow it."

Deng Xiaoping was then playing a very active and increasingly powerful role behind the scenes. He held no official position since the Tiananmen incident. But with Hu Yaobang, Luo Ruiqing, and others who represented a bold new program of reform, he worked to change the ominous political situation that prevailed after Mao's death.

Initially, Hu Yaobang played the pivotal, public role, paving the way for the rise of Deng himself and the policy of economic reform. In the spring of 1977, Hu began to undercut the two "as long ases." Newly appointed as vice-president of the Central Committee Party School, Hu proposed two "regardlesses": "All that is not true and all that is wrongly concluded and wrongly handled must be corrected according to facts, regardless of when and under what circumstances it was done, and regardless of which persons at what levels did it." When some people challenged Hu, saying, "What if Mao himself had given his opinion?" Hu replied, "Rehabilitate as usual." Hu organized a special staff to investigate several key cases that Mao had personally handled.

Hu's role was crucial for Deng's reemergence. For in reality the two "as long ases" were two barriers to Deng's return to power. To rehabilitate Deng would require a reevaluation of Mao's verdict on the Tiananmen Square incident.

Hua Guofeng had no intention of seeing Deng return to power. That is one reason why he reiterated, in a March 1977 political report, that Tiananmen was indeed a counterrevolutionary incident and that it was thus important to criticize Deng Xiaoping. "Criticizing Deng Xiaoping and opposing the Rightists' effort to rehabilitate the Tiananmen Square incident were decided by the great leader Mao Zedong, and are necessary."

But Hu had prepared well. At the end of 1978, the Democracy Wall movement broke out in Beijing, decisively interacting with the reform forces in the Party to defeat the "as long as" faction.

Hu was a remarkable figure in the history of the Chinese Communist Party. Though he ultimately failed as a politician, he was genuinely respected and liked, and it was utterly appropriate that his death in 1989 sparked the massive outpouring of popular discontent of the Beijing Spring. The best aspects of the reform policies that emerged after 1979 are associated with his leadership—the most democratic, open-minded, and humane. Hu repeatedly quoted a passage he remembered from Marx: "Once the lightning of thought touches the garden of people that has never been touched before, Germans will be liberated to become human beings." This was something he ardently sought for the Chinese as well. It was a belief deeply held and often passionately expressed, and it made him one of the very few leaders of the Party who never for a moment forgot that true reform required greater democracy and freedom.

Hu had joined the Red Army when he was very young—a "child soldier" whose high-school education made him very much an intellectual in the military. Suspected of being a member of an anti-Bolshevik group and almost shot in the 1940s, he was rescued by Feng Wenbin, an influential Party member from a working-class background, and ultimately found his way to the Central Committee of the Youth League. This early experience crucially shaped the rest of his life, for it made him particularly sensitive to the cases of others wrongly accused. In the mid-1970s, as his power grew, people sought him out to report their mistaken, false, or wrongly judged cases. They came to his house and there he would talk with them, sometimes for hours. Even when he became the general secretary of the Communist Party, he managed to review thousands of letters of ordinary people. In three years, he gave opinions on over two thousand such letters—repeatedly intervening to expose corrupt officials who used their power for personal ends or to protect the corrupt acts of others. His desire to know what was really happening led to constant inspection trips. By the time he was ousted in 1987, he had visited more than sixteen hundred of China's two thousand counties.

Hu was a meticulous and rapid reader. He read Marx and Engels, as well as the classics—from China and other nations. He had read the complete works of Shakespeare and was particularly fond of the memoirs of world leaders. Mao once commented on his style of reading: "Fond of reading, he does not strive for thorough understanding; fond of making speeches, he chatters on forever." But Mao's comment, a warning to Hu, was not really accurate. Among Party leaders, Hu's fondness of and respect for learning were rare; his protection of intellectuals was related to his own love of learning and his innate curiosity about the world around him. These traits made him uneasy with any dogma.

As a person, Hu was perhaps too guileless and kind to equal the ruthlessness and cunning of his opponents. If he thought people, even his most vehement opponents, had been wrongly treated in the past, he would still rehabilitate them. While he was head of the Organization Department in the Party, he rehabilitated Bo Yibo and helped Peng Zhen. Later, both these members of the Gang of the Old played a key role in ousting him.

Though Deng was to support Hu strongly at times, the differences between their positions on reform were evident from the beginning. Hu had early and bluntly proposed the two "regardlesses." Deng, on the other hand, then being rehabilitated, had written a letter to Hua Guofeng and the Party Central Committee proposing that "we must comprehend completely and accurately the system of Mao Zedong Thought." In 1978, after he had resumed his posts, he elaborated on his position in his speech at the Third Plenary Session of the Tenth Party Committee, opposing "taking Mao's words said in isolation as ultimate truths." Compared with the two "as long ases," this was progress. But it smacks of the ideological opportunism that Deng's supporters prefer to call his "pragmatism."

What such "pragmatism" meant was spelled out by another,

quite different Hu, Hu Qiaomu. He put it quite bluntly: All that is correct—including Liu Shaoqi's ideas, which Mao had opposed—belongs to the system of Mao Zedong Thought. All that is wrong, including that which originated in Mao's thought, does not belong to it. But how do we judge what is wrong and right? In case of conflict, Hu would report to Deng, who would issue the final judgment. This was what "complete and accurate understanding" really meant.

Deng has been all too comfortable with people like Hu Qiaomu. Hu Qiaomu, as the historian Li Shu notes, is that typical example of the hypocrite that resulted from Mao's way of "reforming" intellectuals. Hu had been Mao's secretary since the years in Yanan (1937–45) after he had graduated from Qinghua University. He was brilliant at deciphering Mao's intentions—and shaping his writings to conform to them. When Mao advocated that intellectuals should transform their thinking, Hu criticized himself while bursting into tears, "purifying" his soul. Mao praised Hu Qiaomu as an intellectual who had made his soul most beautiful. And Hu, alone among Mao's secretaries, so trimmed his ways to Mao's shifting positions that he still survives today.

When Deng first returned to office in 1974, Hu Qiaomu worked for him. But when Deng was criticized, Hu made a self-criticism for following Deng and wrote reports on him to Mao's wife, Jiang Qing, who later circulated these critical materials within the party as evidence of Deng's criminal acts. When Mao died in 1976 and the Gang of Four was arrested, Hu made yet another tearful self-criticism, asking Wang Zhen and Deng Liqun to put in a good word for him with Deng. Deng forgave him, calling him "spineless, but not a betrayer," and saying that "he is the first pen inside the Party; we should let him resume work." Thus, Hu Qiaomu returned to Deng Xiaoping's side.

Deng's personality was all too susceptible to flattery such as Hu Qiaomu's. But there are other personality traits that set him apart from Hu Yaobang as well. Hu Yaobang seemed remarkably free of the ruthlessness of character so much a part of the exercise of power in China. This has never been Deng's problem: Mao had warned him when he was returned to power in 1974, "Hide your needle within cotton."

The essence of autocracy, Marx once said, is the tendency to look down on others, to treat them as subhuman. This is the core of Deng's character. His contempt for people's dignity and integrity is astonishing. It permeates his statements and his "pragmatism." When he sentenced Wei Jingsheng and Fu Yuehua for their role in the 1978–79 Democracy Wall movement, he said, "We must never release those that we have captured." Releasing them would only indicate weakness. "China has such a big population," he said in the mid-1980s, "it doesn't matter if we kill a few hundred thousand!" "Even for those that we do not kill, we should cancel their registrations, and expel them from Beijing, never to be allowed to return." When confronted with the democracy movement, he said, "We must get rid of the weed by the root," "Get rid of the evil once and for all," and "Kill two hundred thousand in exchange for twenty years of stability!"

Nothing could be further from Hu Yaobang's temperament. He was a visionary, an idealist thinker.

For a time, this served Deng's purposes.

THE DEMOCRACY WALL MOVEMENT AND THE TRIUMPH
OF THE PARTY REFORMERS, 1978–79

Just as the Central Work Conference began to meet in November 1978, preparatory to the Third Plenary Session of the Eleventh Party Committee, the Democracy Wall movement broke out in Beijing. For several months during the winter of 1978–79, near the intersection of Xidan Street and Changan Avenue, *dazibao,* big-character posters, suddenly began to appear. People came to discuss, debate, and to post their views. Young people who had been through the Cultural Revolution and had witnessed so many of the seamy aspects of Chinese society and the Party quickly became the main force behind the movement. They posted political essays, poetry, and cartoons—depicting the injustices of the Cultural Revolution and then rapidly spreading to questions of the policies of Chairman Mao. Political and literary publications started to circulate privately.

When the Democracy Wall movement began, Hu and Deng were temporarily allied. Hu supported the movement out of deep conviction, but Deng did so largely out of convenience, a useful way to put pressure on those he wished to remove from power.

The immediate spark that led to Democracy Wall reveals just how close the interaction is between popular protest and struggles within the Party. Wang Dongxing had summarily ordered the journal *China Youth* to cease distributing articles questioning the Tiananmen Square verdict. "That the Tiananmen Square incident was counterrevolutionary was decided by Mao. It therefore must not be rehabilitated," Wang said.

The staff of the journal did not comply, instead posting the printed articles on the walls. People gathered in large crowds to read the posters, and criticism rapidly spread, focusing on Wang Dongxing.

Few people offered a more appropriate target for popular discontent with the dogmatism and doctrinaire ways of the past than Wang. Wang had risen to prominence during the Cultural Revolution, when he was in charge of Mao Zedong's security force. He was trusted and promoted by Mao amid the various "court" struggles of the time. The garrison troops under Wang's control had arrested the Gang of Four, making possible Hua Guofeng's greatest accomplishment. Wang had not sought to be emperor. But he wanted to be the pope who crowns him. He often said, "Chairman Mao is satisfied with what Chairman Hua did. He said, 'Hua is not foolish. I like someone who claims that he does not have great talent.' Deng Xiaoping had his try, but he was not nearly as good as Chairman Hua." Wang Dongxing also managed to set himself up as the legitimate person to propagate Party theory. He considered himself the only legitimate heir to Mao Zedong's theory on the Cultural Revolution. He said, "Who knows about the history of the Cultural Revolution? Premier Zhou and Kang Sheng have died. Chen Boda and Jiang Qing were arrested. Chairman Hua came to the Central Committee late, so only I know the facts. I will talk to you about it when I get a chance."

When Mao Zedong was alive, though, Wang Dongxing did not dare to suggest he was qualified to speak about theory. He was merely Mao's housekeeper. But in the last years of Mao's life, when Mao could not go out much and keep in touch with the outside world, this housekeeper became an increasingly important person. He not only controlled the Office of the Central Committee and Mao's bodyguard, the elite 8341st Garrison troop, but also access to Mao. He strongly influenced what Mao said and did. Even when Jiang Qing, Mao's wife, wanted to see Mao, she had to get his approval.

But after Mao died, Wang was no longer satisfied with controlling administrative and military power; he wanted to control theory. Even though he knew nothing about it, Wang was fully aware of the importance of monopolizing theory in the inner-Party struggles. Inside the Communist Party, whoever controls theory has the "truth" and gains decisive power in any political struggle. Wang Dongxing wanted to control theory in just this sense. He was in charge of the committee for the editing and publication of Mao Zedong's works, the theory group of the Central Committee, and the propaganda function of the newspapers and journals. Of course he did not allow any one to challenge the two "as long ases." The fact that *Chinese Youth* dared to try to rehabilitate the Tiananmen Square incident of 1976 was intolerable to him.

But he had been outmaneuvered; his power was ebbing. As soon as *Chinese Youth* was on Democracy Walls, Feng Wenbin (himself the assistant educator at the Party School), who was assisting Hu Yaobang in his work at the Party School of the Central Committee, reported this to Marshal Ye Jianying and Deng Xiaoping. Marshal Ye, though personally quite loyal to Mao, wanted to open China up to reform and more democratic ways. He was central both to the arrest of the Gang of Four and to the strong support for Democracy Walls, which he spoke of as a model for a people's democracy. Deng Xiaoping, for his part, had consolidated significant power behind the scenes. The stage was thus set at this pivotal 1978 meeting for a major shift in power. The Democracy Wall movement decisively shifted the scales against Wang Dongxing and ultimately Hua Guofeng.

As is usually the case with such meetings, the speeches of Hua Guofeng and Ye Jianying, along with the resolutions, had all been prepared beforehand—in this case under the theory group under Wang Dongxing's leadership. The original intentions of the organizers of the session were:

—First, to stick to the "continuing the revolution under the dictatorship of the proletariat" and Hua Guofeng's guideline at the Eleventh Central Committee: "Rule the country by grasping the key link"—which is class struggle.
—Secondly, shift the focus of the Party's work to the building of the Four Modernizations.

These two goals in reality conflicted with each other. It had been more than two years since the smashing of the Gang of Four. During these two years, Wang Dongxing's theory group drafted many speeches and articles, the central theme of which was to propagate the theory of "continuing the revolution under the dictatorship of the proletariat." They successfully associated this theory with the name of Hua Guofeng. Their formula was this: Mao Zedong's greatest contribution to Marxism was to create the theory of continuing the revolution. The only reason Hua Guofeng was in his position was that he stuck to and safeguarded this theory. Thus it was impossible for him to alter this theoretical position. But unlike the theory group under Wang, Hua Guofeng had practical work experience. He understood that after the fall of the Gang of Four, shifting the focus to realizing the Four Modernizations was highly popular. Therefore, Hua sought to combine these two conflicting goals. But he could not do so.

In some ways, Hua's two goals do not seem much different from Deng's. Had not Deng only changed "continuing the revolution" to "opposing bourgeois liberalization"? But Hua was undoubtedly far more constricted by his Maoist past. As for the Gang of the Old, they opposed Hua Guofeng. Their power had been reduced by the Cultural Revolution. He had prospered from it—and for that they could not forgive him. As a consequence, they were quite willing in 1978 to temporarily support Hu Yaobang, who had fought the hardest for Deng's rehabilitation. Some of the Gang of the Old even tolerated the Democracy Wall movement—as long as it was useful.

When Feng Wenbin demanded that the Democracy Wall movement be allowed to continue and that the special investigative group of the Central Committee headed by Wang Dongxing be disbanded, he was supported by a majority. Hua Guofeng's opening speech, calling for a shift from class struggle to economic construction, was largely set aside, as participants were swept up in the various questions posed by the Democracy Walls.

The excitment and ferment were extraordinary. These issues had not been openly discussed for well over ten years. So many questions were raised, so many things said that were on the minds of both the leaders in the party and among the population of Beijing: it was an explosive moment. Calls for democracy were repeatedly voiced on Democracy Walls. And within the Party itself, demands rose to rehabilitate the victims of past persecutions. For a time these two demands reinforced each other, for rehabilitation of officials unjustly punished cut to the quick the rationale of the Cultural Revolution—and raised the question of how to evaluate Chairman Mao himself.

To those in the Party, few cases were more important than those of Peng Dehuai and Tao Zhu.

Peng Dehuai had been highly popular and was probably the most courageous military official in the Party's history. Mao had himself once written a poem praising him: "Who dares to hold the giant sword on a horse? There is only one general Peng." But when Peng had openly criticized Mao's policies after the Great Leap Forward, Mao had condemned him.

Tao Zhu also suffered harsh attacks. He had been the number-four person at the start of the Cultural Revolution, after Mao Zedong, Lin Biao, and Zhou Enlai. But because of his conflicts with Chen Boda and Jiang Qing, he was dismissed early in 1967 and later labeled a traitor and persecuted to death.

In addition, there was the particularly sensitive question of the "sixty-one-member traitors' clique," which included Peng Zhen and Bo Yibo. Sixty-one of them had gotten out of prison by writing confessions, for the most part rituals to which the Party had previously agreed.

The Party now wanted to use the services of some of these old, highly experienced cadres. These cases became one of the most intensely debated issues at the Working Conference precisely because these people had all been highly influential in the Party's history. Their convictions had all been the will of Mao himself. To reevaluate them was to reevaluate the very history of the Party—indeed, of Mao himself.

Wang Dongxing fought to prevent such rehabilitations.

But both within the party and without, the demand for rehabilitations grew—so loudly did it burst forth that the majority approved the rehabilitation of all of them.

Nor was it only on this issue that participants of the Working Conference and the activists of Democracy Walls were indirectly supporting each other. Although the criticisms of Mao raised in the Democracy Walls eventually became quite sweeping, the criticisms at first were not much different from those shared by senior officials in the Party. His policies before 1956 were largely seen as positive. The famous *dazibao* put up by the young people from Guizho was the earliest to affirm that 70 percent of Mao's work was positive, 30 percent negative. That was what Deng said at the Party meetings: "Mao said himself that he would be satisfied with a 70-percent–30-percent division. As for me, I would be happy with 60 percent achievements and 40 percent mistakes."

What insiders and outsiders alike agreed on was their vehement opposition to the two "as long ases" of Hua Guofeng and Wang Dongxing. Under the pressure of this alliance, symbolized by the growing criticism of Mao, Hua Guofeng and Wang Dongxing's alliance broke down. The Democracy Walls as well as the Party meetings all attacked Wang Dongxing and tried to get Hua to change his stance. The strategy worked. Hua agreed to oust Wang Dongxing, and he himself announced that he would give up the two "as long ases."

The alliance of democratic forces within the Communist Party and without in 1978 turned this meeting into a milestone in Chinese history. The process of reform and the opening to the world could not have happened without it. It was this link of inner and outer which unleashed the various forces that augmented the most progressive aspects of the reform that followed.

The Democracy movement in 1989 ultimately lacked this basic dynamic. The link between inner and outer remained broken. And this, as we shall see, provides a key into understanding its brutal ending. For China is still a Party-ruled state: there is no political power but the Communist Party. But the Party is not monolithic; its conflicting currents are of enormous importance to any popular force developing in Chinese society. If democratic forces outside the Party cannot receive effective support from those within, they can hardly realize any political change.

REVOLUTION AND REACTION WITHIN THE PARTY

After 1978, the conflict between the pro- and anti-reform forces within the Party took a new form. Wang Dongxing, the main ideological representative of the old, antireform forces, lost power. Hua Guofeng's influence was gradually diminished. A second power center formed around Deng Xiaoping.

Deng adopted a special strategy to gain control. On the surface, he did not take power. In his speeches, he still used phrases such as "the Central Committee led by Chairman Hua Guofeng." At the 1978 session, Deng resumed his positions of vice-chairman of the Party Central Committee, vice-chairman of the Military Commission, and vice-minister of the State Council. His speech was divided into three sections, titled

"Chairman Mao," "Chairman Hua," and "Myself." The central theme of the speech was, first, to confirm "the system of Mao Zedong Thought," to "have a complete and accurate understanding of Mao Zedong Thought"; second, to recognize Hua Guofeng's historical accomplishments and leadership position; and third, to announce that he was empowered to cooperate with Ye Jianying to assist Hua Guofeng to lead the whole country.

Yet in fact he was already doing more than assisting Hua: he was acting as if he were the center of leadership. In 1989, after the June 4 massacre, he revealed his true thoughts when he said, "The Third Plenary Session of the Eleventh Central Committee [in 1978] formed a new leadership organization—that is, the second generation of leadership. Any organization must have a core, without which it cannot stand. The core of the first generation of leadership was Chairman Mao. I am in fact the core of the second generation of leadership."

Deng Xiaoping did not claim titles such as chairman of the Party, general secretary, or prime minister. Furthermore, he repeatedly declined offers of the highest position. Later on, he even stopped being a member of the Central Committee. But he used the general secretary and the president of the country as his vice-presidents. Regardless of the form, Deng gathered all the powers of the Party, the government, and the army unto himself.

The story of Deng's rise to power is inseparable from the course of the reform movement and the shape it took. During the two years Hua Guofeng continued as Party chairman—from the Third Plenary Session of the Eleventh Central Committee in December 1978 to the Central Committee's working meeting in December 1980—Deng Xiaoping strongly supported the reform forces headed by Hu Yaobang.

At first, this meant Deng supported the Democracy Wall movement. But by the beginning of 1979, it had already exceeded what conservatives in the Party could tolerate. Even some proreform members of the Party felt that too much political freedom was being demanded. Hu Yaobang approved of the demands, but not enough reformers agreed with him, so they did not stand up and protect the Democracy Walls strongly enough.

And Deng knew how to appeal to the Chinese people so that they would place their hopes on his own personal role. He directed his ire at one of the most outspoken young editors of the underground journals, the young worker Wei Jingsheng, whose wall poster, "Democracy, the Fifth Modernization," quickly became famous. The Four Modernizations—modernizing agriculture, industry, science, and defense—were not enough, he wrote. There had to be democracy as well. Wei accused Deng Xiaoping of being an autocrat, and warned that without democracy, economic growth would encounter insurmountable obstacles.

Wei touched an even more sensitive nerve, however. He had dared to raise an issue of foreign policy—Deng's attack on Vietnam. That attack, as Deng knew, had not gone well. And precisely because Deng was so vulnerable on that issue, Wei's public criticisms infuriated him.

Unlike Hu Yaobang, Deng had had enough of the "chaos" of the Democracy Walls. In a speech drafted by Hu Qiaomu, he spoke of the need to stick to the Four Cardinal Principles— to uphold socialism, the dictatorship of the proletariat, the leadership of the Communist Party of China, and Marxism-

Leninism–Mao Zedong Thought. This pivotal speech marked Deng's own endorsement of the theoretical underpinnings of all the later antirightist attacks.

Though Deng was to waver back and forth on this issue in the coming years because he did not want to jeopardize his economic reforms and opening to the world, he had given the approval that the antirightist groups needed to launch their ideological campaigns. Initially, Deng remained quite steadfast in pushing his reform. He proposed continued discussion of the proposition that "practice is the only criterion of truth"—the slogan that underlay much of Hu Yaobang's experimental openness in politics as well as in economics. But from the time Deng censured the increasingly critical spirit animating the Democracy Walls, at the time of China's attack on Vietnam in February 1979, he was ideologically aligned in this critical way with the Gang of the Old.

At times, Deng took quite progressive steps. In February 1980 at the Fifth Plenary Session of the Eleventh Central Committee, Deng proposed that the lifelong appointments of the Party and county leaders be abolished. He sought ways to open up leadership positions to younger people. In May of the same year, he also accepted the suggestion of Li Weihan, a former director of the Department of the United Front of the Party Central Committee, to launch a struggle against "feudalism" within the Party and society, and give up such old slogans as "Foster proletarian thoughts and destroy bourgeois thoughts," which he had himself proposed to the Communist Youth League in 1956.

In response, in April and May 1980, conservatives such as Hu Qiaomu, Deng Liqun, and Wei Guoqing announced, at a series of meetings in the Propaganda Department of the

Central Committee and the General Political Department of the Army, that they would launch an attack on the policies of ideological liberalization. They reiterated the very slogans Deng had dropped, such as "Foster proletarian thoughts and destroy bourgeois thoughts." Hu Yaobang, among others, led a sharp denunciation of such regressive ideological steps. "The most important task in ideology today," he bluntly stated, "is to eliminate the influence of feudalism—both within the Party and in society, and gradually to reform every system with a view toward eliminating the influence of feudalism."

"Feudalism" was the key word. It suggested that the political structure itself had to be profoundly altered. At times Deng seemed quite aware of this. In August 1980, he appeared to side with Hu Yaobang and other reformers in his report to an enlarged meeting of the Politburo, *Reform of the Party and the Country's Systems.* China's problems, Deng insisted, came from the powerful grip of feudalism. And this was augmented by the highly concentrated power of the leaders historically associated with the Communist International—that is, with Stalinism. Mao had not solved this problem; indeed, he had totally disregarded minimal legal restraints on capricious and arbitrary acts. But the problem, Deng noted, was not simply that of an individual. "I am not saying that the individuals were not responsible for their acts, but that the question of the system is more fundamental, universal, and unchanging. If we do not persist in reforming the present system, the serious problems that appeared in the past could still be repeated in the future." Even today, after the Tiananmen massacre, Deng partially acknowledges the consequences of the concentration of power in his own hands: "I realize that I have played too big a part.

This is not good for the country and the Party; someday, it could be dangerous."

Though Deng saw the systemic aspect of the problem, he refused to really confront it. To do so might cut too directly into his own power base. That is why he could, with one hand, support Hu Qiaomu's attacks and emphasize the Four Cardinal Principles, while at the same time continuing to seek economic reform and limited political change.

But this meant that the political change must be very limited indeed. As early as 1980 at the Working Conference of the Central Committee, a turning away from political reform was ominously suggested by the emergence of a new anti-reform clique. It was a group Deng could not ignore, and one from which he could never really free himself—unless he were to lead a major political movement of reform, for which he had no deep inclination. The core of the new group was another of the Gang of the Old, Chen Yun. Of all the Old Men, he alone had the stature to challenge Deng.

Born into a family of workers employed by the Commercial Press, Chen Yun was one of the three representatives of the Chinese Communist Party at the Communist International (with Wang Ming and Kang Sheng). After he returned to Yanan, he was the head of the department of the Central Committee that was in charge of personnel matters and organizational discipline for a long time. Later he was appointed one of the five secretaries of the Secretariat of the Central Committee (the others were Mao Zedong, Liu Shaoqi, Zhou Enlai, and Zhu De). At the Eighth Party Congress in 1956, he was elected vice-chairman of the Party. His qualifications and position were thus considerably higher than those of Deng Xiaoping.

After the founding of the People's Republic of China, he was in charge of economic construction, and he played a decisive role in the Stalin-style planned economy.

Surrounding Chen Yun in the new antireform clique were people like Wang Zhen, Deng Liqun, Hu Qiaomu, Yao Yilin, and Bo Yibo. Chen himself realized that a frontal criticism of Deng would not work; he knew how deeply reform was on the agenda of the Party Congress. But he also knew how vulnerable Deng and other Communist leaders would be to certain criticisms. So his strategy, quickly adopted by his followers, was to focus on specific questions—such as pointing to the dangerous implications for socialism of the Solidarity movement in Poland and how changes in China might foster such developments in China. He warned of the dangers of the annual deficit. He challenged the sweeping ways the leadership had reevaluated Mao's achievements and mistakes.

Chen Yun then openly proposed, in a speech drafted by Hu Qiaomu and Deng Liqun for the December 1980 working conference, that China must oppose liberalization. He advocated a policy of "controlling demands and stabilizing prices; striving for stability at the cost even of some growth; stressing adjustment and slowing down reform; centralizing power on major issues, and decentralizing it on small ones." He proposed that current political and economic reforms be stopped on all fronts, and a return be made to a highly centralized, planned economy.

Meanwhile, Hu Qiaomu and Deng Liqun also drafted a speech for Deng Xiaoping, expressing "total agreement with Chen Yun's views on opposing bourgeois liberalization and adjusting economic work." Deng Liqun also went to the Party School of the Central Committee and made a special-topic report on Chen Yun's ideas on economy, which lasted for four days. In his report, he rejected the reform policies enacted since the Third Plenary Session of the Eleventh Central Committee.

Chen Yun's policy of "slowing down of reform" was not totally effective in the economic realm, simply because the momentum of agricultural reform had become irreversible. The agricultural crisis Chen Yun predicted did not happen, but the economic reforms slowed in the cities. And partly because of Chen's influence, political reform stagnated after 1981. After the movement against liberalization in 1981 and 1982, Deng Liqun took over the Propaganda Department. Wang Zhen took over the Party School. Except for the *People's Daily,* headed by Hu Jiwei and Wang Ruoshui, and the Association of Writers and Artists headed by Zhou Yang, all other organs of theory and propaganda had been taken over by antireform forces.

In 1983, the antireform faction started a campaign against spiritual contamination. First they criticized the humanism and theory of alienation proposed by Zhou Yang and Wang Ruoshui. Then they criticized the freedom of the press and the orientation of the papers advocated by Hu Jiwei. They were getting ready to take over all power in the realms of culture and the media.

The campaign against spiritual contamination was initially supported by Deng Xiaoping. But Wang Zhen, Deng Liqun, and Hu Qiaomu were too eager, and went too far too fast. They could not wait to push this campaign from the ideological realm to the realms of the economy, science, and technology. They spoke also of launching a campaign in the countryside. This created great confusion. Some people thought the Cultural Revolution might return.

92

People at lower levels of the Party throughout the country were loud in their complaints. Hu Yaobang, Zhao Ziyang, Wan Li, and Fang Yi (all of them members of the Politburo) disagreed with what Wang Zhen, Deng Liqun, and Hu Qiaomu did. Wan Li was the first to say there must be no confusion in the countryside. Fang Yi followed by saying there was no spiritual contamination in the realm of science and technology. Zhao Ziyang said that the campaign must not affect economic work.

Before Hu Yaobang left for a visit to Japan, he was able to paper over the confusion and tension that Deng Liqun and the others had created. The situation for reform became a little better. The Third Plenary Session of the Twelfth Central Committee passed a resolution in 1984 on urban economic reform and decided to open fourteen coastal cities to foreign investors. However, the session did not deal with political reform—an omission that only further aided the rise of an economy in which bureaucrats lived on the basis of a combination of corrupt power and a semicommodity economy.

Under these circumstances, Deng Xiaoping temporarily revoked his support for the antireform faction, and said he would dismiss Deng Liqun from his position as head of the Propaganda Department. Beijing residents drank to celebrate. But when this news was reported by the Voice of America, Deng said, "I do not take my orders from the Voice of America" and rescinded the order. Deng Liqun resumed his position as head of the Propaganda Department. As for Wang Zhen, he was still Deng's crony. Deng once said of him, "Wang Zhen is a cannon. Sometimes he has aimed badly, but he is still a lovely cannon."

———

The process of reform in the following years had this see-saw quality, first being pushed forward, then restrained. For the reformers, 1985 was the worst year since 1979. The Disciplinary Committee of the Party Central Committee was finally turned over to the antireform forces under Chen Yun. It had always been very weak and hesitant in dealing with the corrupt elements and criminals within the Party, but in 1985 it showed great efficiency and determination in persecuting the reformers. Two of the most resolute reformers—the Party secretary of Fujian Province, Xiang Nang, and Lei Yu, a prefectural commissioner on Hainan Island—were removed from their posts. Many competent managers and officials who successfully advocated reform in industries were demoted, censored, even put into prison. Hu Yaobang had to retreat step by step during this year. He even published a speech in which he denounced freedom of the press as bourgeois ideology. Deng Xiaoping decided to cancel the Party membership of two prominent intellectuals—the famous astrophysicist Fang Lizhi and the veteran writer Wang Ruowang. In the meantime, the Central Disciplinary Committee was also investigating Liu Binyan.

By 1986, the situation was becoming increasingly difficult. Discontent was growing among the Chinese, and was to burst forth late in the year in student protests that ultimately led to Hu Yaobang's fall.

Early that year, Hu once again tried to encourage democratic reforms. He republished Deng's 1980 speech "On the Reform of the Party's and the Country's Systems," because its attack on feudalism provided the codewords for indirectly supporting limited political reform—in Deng's eyes, at least, just enough reform to promote some of his economic policies.

But in 1986, Deng had even less interest in political reform than he had in 1980. This became graphically apparent in September during the Sixth Session of the Twelfth Central Committee. Lu Dingyi, who had headed the Propaganda Department of the Central Committee before the Cultural Revolution and was an outspoken critic of the mistakes of the Cultural Revolution, argued that opposing liberalization had never played a positive role in the history of the Chinese Revolution. That was too much for Deng. He retorted, "Regardless of what happened in the past, opposing liberalization now is a political necessity—we must oppose it for at least twenty years!" Later, after discussing it with Hu Qiaomu, Deng changed his words to "opposing liberalization for seventy years, until the middle of the next century."

If Deng had wanted democratic reforms, there were many Party members he could have turned to for support. There were old revolutionaries like Lu Dingyi and Zhou Yang who supported a wide range of reforms and had been among the first to analytically dissect Mao's mistakes. But Deng chose to turn away from them. There was Hu Jiwei, a well-known journalist whose advocacy of freedom of the press offered hope for correcting the growing problems in the reform movement through greater public discussion. Deng no longer listened to his advice. Li Chang had fought to rehabilitate countless people; Yu Guangyuan was a skilled economist who could have countered many of Chen Yun's ideas.

But all such people were abandoned by Deng Xiaoping. Meanwhile, Deng increasingly surrounded himself with anti-reformist cronies. They hovered around him, flattered him, and in the byzantine court politics of China, were always there to whisper into Deng's ear, slandering courageous and out-spoken reformers who Deng feared might be undercutting his own position.

THE TRAGIC DEMISE OF HU YAOBANG'S REFORM

After the New Year of 1987, Deng barely spoke for two days. He paced to and fro inside his room, muttering to himself, "It is true that I did not fail in the hands of the Gang of Four. Don't let me fail in the hands of Hu Yaobang." The fact that January 4 was a Sunday slipped his mind. Seeing his children at home, he sent them off to work, to get them out of the house. The reason was that Deng was gathering Zhao Ziyang, Yang Shangkun, Wang Zhen, Bo Yibo, and Peng Zhen at his house to discuss ousting Hu Yaobang. This was what became known as "the decision by the Standing Committee in Beijing." In fact, though, among those present, only Deng and Zhao were members of the Standing Committee. Of the other three members of the committee, Hu Yaobang and Chen Yun did not participate, and Li Xiannian was still in Shanghai.

Deng's mutterings seem absurd; Hu had no designs on Deng Xiaoping. However, upper-level political life in the Central Committee is very much like court politics in feudal China. When Wang Zhen and Deng Liqun constantly slandered Hu Yaobang to Deng, it was hard for him not to believe them.

But the real reason Deng wanted to oust Hu is that Hu had steadfastly kept to his more radical stance on political and ideological reform. He never wavered or considered them mere tactical steps, as did Deng Xiaoping. After his economic reforms in 1986 had apparently not borne results, Deng had momentarily revived the question of political reform. Hu took his words seriously, or at least hoped to use them to encourage reform efforts, so he republished Deng's 1980 speech.

Deng further led him on, saying that he planned to retire even further from the political stage. "I will retreat completely. I will no longer be chairman of the Military Commission. You retreat halfway and play my role. Zhao Ziyang should be chairman of the country, and we should let young people be prime minister and general secretary." Hu believed Deng. And he hoped it would set a good example for generations to come of how leadership could be changed and how important it was to put an end to the system of holding leadership positions for life.

Others read Deng's mind much better. Having heard the news, Wang Zhen, the "lovely cannon" of the ad hoc "Standing Committee," hurried to the Party's School auditorium and made a strong speech against Hu Yaobang, saying, "Whoever wants Deng to bow out, the whole Party will be against him."

This sealed Hu's fate.

Another factor contributed to Hu's political demise. Believing that political reform at last required serious steps against corruption, Hu took an extraordinary step. He obtained the appropriate papers for the arrest of Hu Qiaomu's son for embezzling over three million yuan. To move so decisively against the corruption of the children of the leaders sent a seismic shock throughout that elite. Hu Qiaomu and his son, of course, formed an immediate alliance with others to fight for their survival. And Hu Qiaomu tearfully threw himself on Deng's mercy. Once again, his tears proved effective.

Hu Yaobang confronted another difficult challenge from a quite different front. Zhao Ziyang now moved against him as well. His role in Hu's removal was a critical one. For five and a half years after 1981, the Deng-Zhao-Hu system publicly appeared to work effectively. Sometimes Deng told foreign guests, "Even if heaven fell, there would be Hu Yaobang and Zhao Ziyang to hold it up."

But Zhao was moving to remove Hu, seeing him not as an ally but a troublesome rival. Zhao held that the economic realm all but belonged to himself personally. So he turned to those who most opposed reform and aligned himself with Chen Yun, Deng Liqun, and Hu Qiaomu to attack Hu.

He secretly wrote to Chen Yun and Deng Xiaoping, claiming that he could not effectively cooperate with Hu. Whenever Hu visited other cities, Zhao argued, he made speeches that interfered with Zhao's economic directives and planning. How could he hope to produce effective economic results this way? And Hu had a big mouth, Zhao bluntly concluded. If you, the old respected leaders, don't solve this problem before you die, who will control him? So it was imperative, Zhao wrote, to solve this problem: In essence, he was saying they should dismiss Hu from his position as general secretary of the Communist Party.

The letter was not made public until January 1987, when Hu was removed. But as Zhao himself said at a Party meeting before the Spring Festival, the Central Committee had already decided to oust Hu before the student demonstrations of 1987 had erupted. The decision was to have been announced at the Thirteenth Party Congress in October, but the eruption of the student movement precluded further delay.

For the antireform forces, the ouster of Hu was a major victory, greatly expanding their power. The era of reform had in fact ended.

THE HISTORIC OPPORTUNITY THAT ZHAO ZIYANG LOST

Having succeeded in his maneuvering, however, Zhao was in a dilemma. He was now isolated.

After Hu's ouster in 1987, Zhao proposed the so-called "two basic points": to oppose liberalization in politics, and to reform the economy and open it to the outside world. His advisors called this the "new authoritarianism," a combination of autocratic political government and liberal economic methods.

Deng and Zhao had a short honeymoon period while promoting Zhao's "two basic points." But the economic problems themselves could not be handled by such methods. The "marriage" of autocratic power to a "free economy" was in fact a honeymoon of power and money. Whoever had power would be able to use the price difference between the planned economy and the market economy to make huge profits. That is the root of the rampant corruption today— and it still continues to grow with frightening speed. This combination of power and money, furthermore, led to an ever more direct conflict between the people and the privileged class. As power and money were so directly combined, the struggle in the Party rapidly intensified and now involved both.

The fate of Zhao in 1989 resembles that of Hu Yaobang two years earlier. Neither escaped the fate of being the heir.

Just as he had two years earlier, Deng Xiaoping announced that he would resign. He told everyone, including foreign guests, that he would give up the chairmanship of the Military Commission to Zhao Ziyang. Thereupon, the antireform forces gathered again, this time to oppose Zhao Ziyang. But at first they were not very effective, as Deng balanced Zhao against the antireform forces.

In 1988, when General Jaruzelski of Poland visited China, he said to Deng Xiaoping, "You are the chairman of the Military Commission. But General Secretary Zhao Ziyang and Yang Shangkun are all vice-chairmen of the Military Commission. How should I understand the relationship between the Chinese army and the Party and the state?"

Deng replied, "This is the Chinese way." Later he said, "Don't always turn to me for military affairs."

But who should one turn to? Deng did not say.

Since Yang Shangkun was the vice-chairman of the Military Commission, he felt that he should take over some military matters. He made a note on one document saying that anyone who wanted to discuss military affairs should see him. This apparently displeased Deng Xiaoping. So when an opportunity arose, Deng Xiaoping told foreigners that Zhao Ziyang should be in charge of the army, since he was the first vice-chairman.

In China these major issues are not discussed at formal meetings of the Central Committee. What is discussed at those meetings is trivial. Major issues are all decided before the meetings. And they are often determined by Deng Xiaoping according to his whims. He has often told foreigners first, as he did with the price reform of 1988.

Then in April 1989, Hu Yaobang died.

People's grief was spontaneous. Perhaps in their heart of hearts, they still harbored some vague hope that someday Hu would play a major role in promoting democratic reform in China. But now all hope had been dashed, and sadness and resentment rose to the surface. This can be clearly seen in a poem that appeared at Beijing University one day after Hu's death:

> An honest man died,
> Yet hypocrites live;
> A warm-hearted man died,
> And cold-hearted ones bury him.
> Empty talk, favors, mah-jongg, bridge, and new
>   authoritarianism:
> Reform and its death.
> This world is truly a new labyrinth.
> Let me ask you, Yaobang,
> Is there still hope for China?

On the morning of April 22, 1989, more than two hundred thousand students were gathered in Tiananmen Square. In order to avoid being shut out by the planned barricades, they had entered the square on the previous evening, and had waited through the long, cold night. The sincerity and warmth there outside the Great Hall of the People made a striking contrast with the coldness and hypocrisy at the official memorial within.

The outpouring of grief quickly focused on the government headed by Prime Minister Li Peng. Though he was the son of martyrs and raised under the guidance of Prime Minister Zhou Enlai and his wife, Deng Yingchao, Li was neither widely respected nor much liked. He had studied in the Soviet Union, and upon returning to China, he quickly worked his way up from managing the Xiaofengman hydroelectric power station in Northeast China to becoming Minister of Electric Power.

101

When the ministries of hydro power and electric power were merged, he became vice-minister. Qian Zhengying, the minister, thought Li did not do a good job as vice-minister. Nor did a wide range of people, including students, believe he was effective when he served on the State Education Commission.

When Hu was removed in 1987, Deng wanted Wan Li to become prime minister. Wan Li, though a reformer, was very close to Deng. In 1975, when Deng first returned to power, Wan had skillfully reorganized China's entire railroad system. Later, as first secretary of Anhui Province, he led sweeping agricultural changes. He had opposed the constant attacks against liberalization. When Hu Yaobang was forced to resign, Wan Li submitted his resignation to Deng. But Deng insisted he stay on, and proposed him as prime minister.

Zhao sided with the Gang of the Old to oppose Wan, and proposed Tian Jiyun instead. But this was voted down.

Deng concluded that only Li Peng was acceptable by all sides. He asked Wan Li to support Li Peng, and Wan Li, loyal to Deng, did so. It was a fateful choice. No one then imagined how fanatical Li Peng could be after he got the full support of the Gang of the Old.

The Gang of the Old was prepared to move decisively against the popular movement. Their aim was to change the balance of power within the Politburo, and when Zhao left for Pyongyang on the afternoon of April 23, they acted.

The influence of Peng Zhen and his supporters, who controlled the Beijing Municipal Committee, was critical. They drafted a report calling the student movement a "rebellion"; the report forced the hand of the Politburo.

Peng Zhen himself was a brilliant organizer, a match for

Deng himself. He had been mayor of Beijing—and had organized the city almost as his own kingdom. He was therefore one of the first people Mao attacked at the beginning of the Cultural Revolution. Though he and his men were purged at the time, his people were able to return to power. Indeed, his organization was so tight that Zhou Enlai repeatedly complained how difficult it was to get anything done in the capital. When Zhou first brought Deng back into favor in 1975, Deng asked what to do about Peng Zhen; Zhou said, "He wouldn't do. He has problems in his background." Ironically, it was Hu Yaobang who had helped Peng Zhen to be rehabilitated.

Once it was ready to act, the Gang of the Old relied on Yao Yilin, a member of the Standing Committee of the Politburo, to coordinate the efforts of Li Peng, Wang Zhen, and Yang Shangkun against Zhao. And to ensure the efforts were effective, the Old Men involved themselves directly in the proceedings of the Standing Committee. Among its five members, only Li Peng and Yao Yilin supported the decision to crack down on the demonstrators. They clearly also favored the hard-line editorial of April 26. Qiao Shi's attitude was wavering and unclear. If the Old Men had not interfered, there would have been no majority in favor of suppression. Only under the immediate pressure of the Gang of the Old was Qiao Shi won over; even Hu Qili did not dare to support Zhao any longer.

Though the Gang of the Old moved to consolidate its position, the student movement quickly developed into a huge democratic force supported by the people of Beijing. And this created a historic opportunity for the reform forces to confront their opponents.

When Zhao Ziyang returned from Korea on April 29, if the Democracy movement had been stopped, his choices would have been clear: either follow the opinion of the "majority" of the Standing Committee of the Politburo and acquiesce in Deng's decision to suppress the "rebellion" and arrest "rebellious elements" and "elements of liberalization," or else resign like Hu Yaobang. Either way, he would have to follow the wishes of Deng and the other members of the antireform alliance.

But as it turned out, the demonstrations were in full swing, demanding democracy. Thus Zhao and other proreform leaders in the Party had a rare opportunity, similar to the one that had faced Hu Yaobang and other reformers ten years before. However, this time the alliance between the democratic forces in society and the proreform forces within the Party was not formed. Why?

Some accuse the students of overstressing independence; they so feared being used by the power blocs within the Party that they did not want to form an alliance, and thus lost their only chance of success. But pursuing an independent political stance does not necessarily exclude a flexible strategy. In May 1989, in Beijing, the alliance of the Democracy movement and the proreform forces within the Party was the only chance for defeating the antireform forces.

But the real reason why the Democracy movement of 1989 failed is that the reformers within the Party were too indecisive, waiting and looking on, wavering and backing up. They, not the students, lost the opportunity.

The reformers within the Party made three major mistakes. First they gave up the initiative for conducting a dialogue with the students to Li Peng and his clique. This was a vital mistake. The key to forming an alliance between the reformers within the Party and the Democracy movement was in grasping the initiative to conduct a dialogue. The dialogue offered by the Li Peng clique was merely a ploy to buy time, and the students never fell for the trick. After Zhao Ziyang returned, he made speeches on May 3 and 4, and was warmly received by the students. He could have taken the initiative then and organized a prestigious and influential group of leaders to conduct a dialogue with the students. That might have been the key to forming an alliance with the Democracy movement, and to obstructing the conspiracies of the antireform forces. But Zhao hesitated and eventually gave way on this key issue. He expressed his wish to meet the students several times, but he was stopped by Li Peng. The crux of the matter was exactly that Zhao should have talked with them whether or not Li Peng agreed.

Second, they gave up the initiative to overcome their opponents through legal procedures. On May 16, Zhao Ziyang told Gorbachev the decision of the First Session of the Central Committee of the Thirteenth Party Congress (November 1987) that Deng Xiaoping would make decisions on the most important issues, thus giving the powers of the general secretary to the "helmsman." During the demonstrations on May 17, there were banners that read: "COME OFF THE STAGE, YOU LAST EMPEROR!" Then on the morning of May 20, Li Peng made a speech in which he threatened to use the army to quell the rebellion, alienating the people completely. From May 16 until the end of May, soldiers were blocked and surrounded by civilians outside Beijing.

During the week between May 16 and May 23, even high-ranking army officials and many Party officials were against military suppression of the movement. This presented an extremely good opportunity for the reformers in the Party to form an alliance with the Democracy movement. As general secretary, Zhao Ziyang had the power to call a general conference of the Central Committee, to enlarge it to include officials of the localities, and to call for discussions to negate Li Peng's speech. He would surely have gotten the support of the majority. He could also have suggested that the vice-chairman of the National People's Congress hold an urgent meeting of the People's Congress, which would surely have ended in ousting Li Peng and producing a very different outcome. By using military airplanes to bring in the members, and by following all the normal procedures of such meetings, these two meetings could have taken place in Beijing within the same day. But Zhao did not do this. Nor did Xi Zhongxun inform Wan Li, who was visiting Canada at that time. Nor did Hu Jiwei and Qin Chuan (the director of the *People's Daily* after Hu Jiwei, and a member of the National People's Congress) personally meet with Zhao to encourage him to do so. Instead, they merely telephoned him. What was especially peculiar was that Zhao asked Yan Mingfu to see Yang Shangkun, hoping that Yan Mingfu would request on behalf of himself a meeting of the Standing Committee of the People's Congress and elect another government.

Yan Mingfu had good connections with the old ones in the Party because of his father, Yan Baohang, a noted democratic personage in China. Yan Mingfu had been labeled a rightist in 1957; after he was rehabilitated in 1979, he worked for the Chinese Encyclopedia Press. Later he was promoted to the Secretariat of the Central Committee.

But apparently Yan Mingfu did not press Yang Shangkun for a meeting. At any rate, no meeting was held. Rather, six Old Men rushed into the Standing Committee of the Politburo, and, by pressuring the other four members, successfully toppled Zhao Ziyang. What a clean move! Truth was on the side of the reformers and the people; lawful right and regular procedures were on the side of the proreform forces. Had the reformers taken the initiative, the conspiracy and the small-scale political coup could have been destroyed. But instead, they lost the initiative and waited to be destroyed. This was Zhao Ziyang's tragedy.

Third, they gave up the initiative of using the modern mass media. One important feature of the Democracy movement of 1989 was that it was significantly located in the media. On May 16, hundreds of editors and journalists from CCTV, the *People's Daily,* and other news agencies took to the streets and held up signs with slogans such as "Oppose the Editorial of April 26!" and "Do Justice to Wrongs Done to the *People's Daily* !" In fact, since May 13 most of the news media refused to be controlled by the Propaganda Department, and took the initiative in providing objective reporting. Yet the proreform forces within the Party did not grasp this opportunity to use the mass media to gain public support for their own legality. They should have publicized urgent meetings of the Central Committee and the People's Congress. They should have had the general secretary and chairman and vice-chairman of the People's Congress, famous scholars, and members of the Standing Committee of the People's Congress speak on TV and radio. In this way, they could have exposed the illegality of the Li Peng government and its proclamation of martial law to the soldiers and the people all over the country.

107

All these mistakes of the prodemocracy forces in the Party, however, were not accidental. The reformers were not united or organized. Zhao Ziyang himself was restricted by the discipline of the Party, and was afraid of being called a "divider." Therefore, he hesitated and wavered. This was always his weakness. His two "basic points" and his theory of new authoritarianism were fatal flaws. He advocated freedom in economics but dictatorship in politics. He did not trust an alliance with the people; instead, he still had illusions about the autocrats' open-mindedness. When he realized that he had fallen out of favor with an autocrat, he still sentimentally sent Yan Mingfu to talk to Yang Shangkun, asking him to go with him to see Deng, so that Deng would express his attitude toward the April 26 editorial. Zhao hoped that Deng would say something like, "We treated the student movement a little too harshly."

If Zhao had not pinned his hope on Deng, Li, and Yang, but concentrated on conducting a dialogue with the students and using their legal rights, as well as the mass media, it would not have been impossible to turn back the hundred thousand soldiers outside Beijing. It is not true that the 1989 Democracy movement was doomed to failure. In fact, the antireform forces were not in any better position than the Democracy movement. Strong forces within the Party and the army were against shooting at the demonstrators. If Zhao Ziyang had taken the initiative, he could have gotten them to speak out and stop the shooting. On the other hand, those who supported shooting hesitated to give the orders. This is why the army could not enter Tiananmen Square for more than two weeks. Even the final order for the massacre was ambiguous. The order to "counterattack in self-defense" could be interpreted in various ways. Different divisions handled the situation very differently. Some shot like madmen, and some did not fire a single shot.

DENG'S LEGACY

On June 9, 1989, after his troops had slaughtered the Democracy movement, Deng analyzed why it happened. "This is no ordinary student movement. This is rebellion," he said. It was a "counterrevolutionary" act. It was "predestined" to occur given the "international big climate" and the "national small climate."

Deng was correct about the inevitability of the clash. But the way he perceived it was totally upside down. His own reforms had helped unleash the very forces in China that were incompatible with his refusal to reform the old autocratic system. When Deng stopped using the word "democratization" and spoke of opposing liberalization, he turned his back on any efforts to find new political ways to shape the emerging forces in China's economic and social life.

The changes during the ten years of reform and economic opening have been enormous. The rural areas will never be the same. The communes have been dissolved; peasants have been given a degree of freedom never before experienced. Over sixty million peasants left the land to work in factories; and the explosion of nonagricultural production in the countryside has permanently altered the old ways.

In the cities, multicentered, semi-independent forces were an inevitable outgrowth of the reform years. Private enterprises could not help but be drawn to the Democracy movement. Nor could old Stalinist planning methods ever again

109

work, though it is questionable that they ever did function effectively. Indeed, disputes about planned economies vs. market systems do not really get to the heart of China's changing economic and political needs.

When the Gang of the Old speak of planning, they have little in the way of past accomplishments to point to. Indeed, too much of that planned economy reflected the whims of Mao and other leaders. As Bo Yibo, one of the Gang of the Old, said in a talk several years ago at the Party School, planning could be the result of quite capricious decisions. Once when he was swimming with Mao in Zhongnanhai right before a meeting at Beidaihe, Mao asked him: "What do you think the iron and steel production will be for this year?" Bo Yibo was just making a turn in the water, and replied casually, "Make a turn"—using a phrase that also means "double." So, to his amazement, he found Mao announcing to the world shortly after that China's iron and steel production would reach 10,700,000 tons—double the 1957 output.

Yet Deng really had no clear conception of the market either. In 1984, it was proposed that "the market adjusted by the state and enterprises led by the market" offered a way to combine planning with the market—to overcome defects of the unplanned economy without any directives. This effort failed—but not for economic reasons. The resistance was political—from the increasingly corrupt bureaucratic system. It did not want a planned economy; it sought only to protect its privileges. The result was no plan—and no really free market either—but rather an out-of-control economy under the rule of a privileged group that was utterly unable to control the rapidly emerging multicentered economic forces.

Intellectuals have changed their attitudes during these years.

They have lost many of their illusions about the leadership—and know far more about the inner history of China's "socialism." Workers are also far more aware of the corruption that permeates almost all aspects of government, the Party, and the state-run enterprises. Many Party members as well are sympathetic to the vigorous new currents of thought and the deep yearning for a political transformation of the old autocratic political ways.

Deng's orders to shoot to kill the protesters will prove effective only in the short run. Too many aspects of China's life have been changed by the very reforms he championed.

While civilians were blocking troops from entering Beijing, they were wearing headbands that said: "DO YOU HAVE 1.1 BILLION SOLDIERS?" That is their answer to Deng's contempt for them. He can arrest, suppress, and build new prisons in remote areas. But no matter how many are built, can they hold us all? Your Ministry of Public Security, your Juridical Department—do they have enough hands to go around?

Deng has made himself the enemy of the Chinese people. And because the people he despises will always be there, generation after generation, they will remember what he did.

3

WHERE IS CHINA HEADED?

THE GANG OF THE OLD

After his June 9 speech was publicized, it became clear that Deng had sided completely with the most reactionary forces within the Party—the Gang of the Old. The order to kill was the joint decision of the eight old autocrats. When Deng praised them in his speech, he was praising himself: "The most favorable condition is that we still have a whole group of old people alive. They have experienced all kinds of hardships, and understand the pros and cons of a situation. They are the most resolute in taking action against the rebellion." These old ones, Deng continued, are very valuable, because "without the support of so many old people in our Party, even the nature of this incident could not have been determined." What exactly was that nature? Deng's answer: "counterrevolutionary rebellion" with the intent to overthrow the Party and the state. From now on, there is no need to distinguish Deng from the rest of the Gang of the Old.

Since 1979, the Gang of the Old had never stopped working. They had tried many times, but without Deng's help they were unable to create much of an uproar. At the beginning of 1987, they achieved their first real victory—getting rid of Hu Yaobang. In 1989, they finally achieved a complete victory— burying Deng's enterprise along with Deng.

However, the two victories were won a bit too late. In both 1987 and 1989, when the Gang of the Old got rid of the two highest leaders of the Communist Party elected through legal procedures and destroyed the Democracy movement in a sea of blood, they had to act illegally. They were no longer members of the Politburo, nor were they even members of the Central Committee. They had no legal status to make these decisions. This point is crucial, for a few years from now, any member of the Communist Party can make an appeal and overthrow all the decisions made in 1987 and 1989. It is understandable why the old ones wanted to win so badly, for their days are numbered. If they did not act now, it might be too late. They are in what we call the stage of the "candle in the wind"—they might be blown out any day. They have fought for their "Red China" for decades. Once their positions were threatened, how could they be at peace?

"I have fought for this land!" they say. And those who fought for the land naturally should be masters of the land. Why must Hu Yaobang go? Because one of the reasons for his "bourgeois liberalization" was that he constantly opposed the system of lifelong leaders. He kept nudging the old ones to give up their chairs. He even wanted to punish the sons and daughters of the old who engaged in illegal activities. And he had already *arrested one!* So it would be extremely dangerous to let him go on as general secretary.

The members of the Gang of the Old, as human beings or as politicians, belong to a species rare in the twentieth century. People with such exceptional experiences and personalities are hard to find except in China. The old ones did not begin to taste the flavor of being "masters of the land" only in 1949. Even in the 1920s, in the Central Soviet Area, and later in the base area during the Anti-Japanese War, and in the Liberated Areas, the Communist Party already had political power, its own army, and people under its jurisdiction. This distinguishes the Chinese Communist Party from parties of other countries. Even Lenin and Stalin did not know the taste of having true power for so long a time. Most members of the Gang of the Old had more than twenty years of war experience. They all appreciate the truth that "power comes from the barrel of a gun." And when the war of liberation was over, they agreed with Mao, who summarized their conception of human lives and happiness in a nutshell: people must "fear neither hardship nor death." The full implications of this slogan were revealed in the battles during the Cultural Revolution: not fearing death meant life was worthless.

Why did the Chinese Communist Party have such an aversion to discussions of humanism and human nature from the 1950s till today? In large part because of the peculiar traditional mentality of the old members and their speaking of class struggle after 1949. Imagine, if people had dignity and self-respect, how could they betray or persecute others at will? If people had love of others, how could they kill "class enemies"? The most "heroic" acts performed by the soldiers who shot and killed unarmed people in Beijing this June could not have been performed by officers and soldiers "poisoned" by humanism. Chinese people, seeing such scenes on TV, could not but compare them with what happened during the Cultural Revolution, when the Red Guards would grab the "criminals" by the hair, push their heads down, and twist their arms behind them so that they writhed in anguish. But now it is the state police that have taken over the role of the Red Guards. Since the Chinese government allowed journalists to take pictures of such scenes, it meant that they wanted to publicize the action. How can there be room for "humanism" in class struggle? As long as we can destroy the morale of our enemies and publicize it through TV, we can let the "elements of rebellion" that lie in wait and those who side with "bourgeois liberalization" see the severity of the Party's "leadership"!

After 1949, the old ones were provided with magnificent residences, even palaces in which emperors used to dwell, and carefully protected with more and more garrison soldiers. When they went out to "inspect," soldiers swarmed around them, cutting them off from ordinary people. What they see on the faces of their secretaries and subordinates is always respectful and docile smiles. What they constantly hear is applause, encouragement, and praise. This in part, of course, is their due reward, they feel, which they have earned with their service. It also makes them feel that they do possess unusual wisdom and foresight. It follows, therefore, that they have only to listen to reports, glance through reference materials—and that is enough. Why actually read books or newspapers? They also have a constant supply of personal luxuries, such as food and cigarettes, so they have no need to have anything to do with the market. When they need to use cash, it is only as a symbolic gesture. The vegetables they eat are cultivated in designated gardens. The water they drink comes from a special channel that connects to Jade Spring Mountain, and has no pollution.

Many of the old ones were not much affected by the Cultural Revolution. Some even continued to hold their original positions, until the fall of the Gang of Four. Only a few were persecuted and became "old cadres who were cruelly persecuted by Lin Biao and the Gang of Four." Of course, no one would ask such unpleasant questions as: Did you do anything between 1949 and 1966 to prevent Mao from making wrong decisions? Are you at least in part responsible for the Cultural Revolution? Nobody asks, and of course it would never occur to them either. Since they were persecuted during the Cultural Revolution, they think this proves they were correct then. After regaining power in 1979, they sought to lead China back to their ideal kingdom of the mid-1960s. Even the economic reform that Deng had started they found quite unacceptable. "What kind of socialism is that?" they asked. The proreform forces headed by Hu Yaobang even wanted political reform— how could that be tolerated? Of course they would support the "four basic principles," especially the principles of sticking to "the leadership of the Party" and sticking to the "dictatorship of the proletariat."

As their peers died off, their relative positions improved. When Mao ceased to be the "head of the family" for the Party and the country, they took over this role with pride, feeling completely justified in doing so. Theirs is a world in which they enjoy all pleasures and live free from all cares, under the old political system protected by the "four basic principles." How could they not like the four basic principles? How could they not oppose the "bourgeois liberalization" that so threatens the status quo?

Cared for by the best doctors, the most advanced medicine that China can provide, these old politicians can expect to "always keep their revolutionary youth." Special *qi gong* experts give them treatments to prolong their lives. But despite all that effort, nature is irresistible. The originally not-too-active minds become more feeble. The originally not-much-used senses become numb and slow; their memory fades. Even though they can hardly put a coherent sentence together, they insist on seeing foreign visitors. Even though they can only work for one hour, they still want to utilize it to assert their power to interfere with government affairs. For they must not be forgotten by the people. And they must not let "the land they have fought for" be destroyed by those who favor "bourgeois liberalization."

One important feature of the clique represented by the old is their attitude toward the people. Who are the people, in their experience? They are a source of soldiers. Once they join the army, people will become docile tools to be manipulated at will. The second kind of people they know is the peasants of the 1920s and 1940s, who were poor and ignorant. These peasants they saw as awaiting their liberation. In return, the peasants would be extremely grateful to them and would do anything that they wanted. After 1949, people on the mainland became the masters of the People's Republic only in theory. Of course, the people have their People's Congress, and they also have "representatives" who are "elected." But the list of candidates is decided by the leaders of the Party, and because of the "superiority of the socialist democracy," candidates were not allowed to compete in an election. Therefore, even though the people had the "right" to elect their representatives, they did not know their candidates and the candidates did not know the people, not to mention being responsible to them. They did not convey people's opinions to the People's Congress (because they never asked for these opinions), nor did they report to the people on discussions in the People's Congress. So the People's Congress became a rubber stamp.

After 1979, their basic relationship with the Communist Party had not changed. Treated as politically unimportant and kept ignorant of state affairs, they were never able to change their passive status. At least this was true until the beginning of the 1970s. The people are the source of productivity, and they are the tools of the class struggles the Party initiated so many times. That is all. It was the old politicians who maintained this state of affairs. And it is natural that these politicians look down upon such a people. At the same time, they distrust the people, afraid that once they become rich, they would not continue along the "socialist road," or they might rebel against the Communist Party. This is why, over the past forty years, not one major resolution was passed in the Party after consulting the people; this is also why the Party has never wanted the People's Congress to become an institution that truly reflects people's wishes; and this is also why the number of Party and government officials grew to twenty times its original size over the past thirty years—in order to control the people with an elaborate system of government.

The Gang of the Old believes in the use of force. Vice-

Chairman Wang Zhen often says, "I have four million troops at my disposal!" (or "I have three million troops at my disposal!" after cutbacks). Over the past ten years, when victims of wrongly judged, false, and mistaken cases came to Beijing, when students took to the streets and demonstrated, when the movement against "bourgeois liberalization" persecuted intellectuals, Wang Zhen always shouted, "I have four (three) million troops at my disposal! Arrest! Kill!" Later the Gang of the Old felt it was not enough to depend on the troops. In 1988, they sent people to Poland and Austria to receive training as antiriot police. When they came back, they would train more people. This clearly shows that they had been making preparations to suppress people for a long time. Unfortunately for them, all they have now is their force and secret agents. They must use these means to suppress more and more people—even many Party members.

Calling the peaceful demonstrations of students and citizens a "counterrevolutionary rebellion" was an excuse for cracking down on them. But if one studies this more carefully, it was not entirely without reason. The Gang of the Old was frightened by what was happening in Tiananmen Square in May. For it is a place where people usually express their gratitude and pledge their loyalty to the old ones, where red flags wave and gongs and drums are sounded in celebration. It has been like this for the past few decades. Even in 1984, when people were celebrating the thirty-fifth anniversary of the People's Republic and Deng's eightieth birthday, Beijing students were still forming flower designs which said, "How are you, Xiaoping!" to show their respect. Now it has become "How foolish you are, Xiaoping!" "How cruel you are, Xiaoping!"

An important factor—unknown to the world but significant in explaining why the Gang of the Old took such brutal measures to suppress the students—is the size of the 1989 Democracy movement. Neither the official Chinese media nor the foreign correspondents (most of whom were based in Beijing) reported demonstrations outside of Beijing and a few big cities. According to the foreign news agencies, there were demonstrations in some thirty cities. But the actual number of cities and towns involved was several times that.

For example, when we hear about demonstrations in Hunan Province, we only hear what happened in the provincial capital, Changsha; but in fact there were demonstrations in prefectural cities like Xiangtan and five or six county towns around it, including Mao Zedong's native town of Shaoshan. After June 4, the demonstrators were even more vehement: all transportation between Xiangtan and Changsha was blocked.

As to Shaanxi Province, we all knew that there were heated demonstrations in the capital city, Xian. But we could hardly conceive that even in the "Sacred Revolutionary Base" of Yanan, students were also demonstrating in the streets, shouting slogans in favor of democracy and against the autocratic rule of the CCP.

In many other provinces the situation was more or less the same. Demonstrations persisted even after the massacre in Beijing. People protested the Party's brutality with greater vehemence than ever.

Most of us hardly had an inkling of these facts, but the Gang of the Old knew about every single demonstration as soon as it took place, because the local security bureaus were directed to report any serious event to Beijing every day. It is easy to imagine the reaction of Deng Xiaoping to these reports piling up before him, several hundred such reports coming every day

123

during the months of May and June. It was unprecedented, not only since the Communist Party took over in 1949, but also in the entire history of China.

That Zhao Ziyang dared to resist Deng Xiaoping and was supported by some important people inside the Party and the military turned the fear of the Old Men into sheer panic. Those who did not live in Zhongnanhai hurried to move there. Later they felt that even Zhongnanhai was not safe, so they moved to the Jade Spring Mountain in the western suburbs of Beijing—a residence built for wartime. Were they afraid of people forcing their way into Zhongnanhai or of being bombed? The feeling that a great catastrophe was imminent and that their very existence was threatened was probably the real motive for them to decide on the massacre as a last resort.

Any normal person would wonder, Before these old men decided to take these drastic measures, did they ever think about how they proposed to rule China afterward? Because the aftermath of the massacre would be too evident: more protests, more repression. Of course these old men went ahead because they all have a blind belief in military force and are out of touch with reality. But there is another reason: these old men are utterly selfish, mean, and hypocritical.

The Chinese Communist Party Central has always proclaimed that they pay a great deal of attention to "political impact"—that is, their image both at home and abroad—and at the same time has advised others to sacrifice their own interests for the interests of the whole nation. But the June 4 massacre made the CCP lose all its respectability with its friends abroad overnight. George Hinton, the U.S. agriculturist who had been on friendly terms with the CCP for fifty years decided to break all his relations with China after the massacre. He even suggested worldwide sanctions to this brutal government, including embargoes of grain exports. But the Gang of the Old didn't seem to care, because any loss incurred would not harm their immediate interest, and their days are in any case numbered.

There is a story that has often been told lately: Two young people were chatting one day on the streets of Beijing. "I feel a strange kind of discomfort," said one. "I'm tired, and lack energy. I don't know why."

"What kind of disease is this? Is it physical or psychological?"

"I just realized yesterday that it is because I have not heard funeral music on the radio for such a long time!"

The people's hope for the death of a few high-level officials has grown stronger over the past few years. Their fears were clearly justified. If only two or three of the Gang of the Old had died a few months earlier, the 1989 spring in Beijing would have had an entirely different outcome.

A NEW KIND OF TERRORISM

China has never experienced the kind of terrorism it is experiencing today. In the past, China's rulers focused on the few opponents who constituted threats to their rule. The Beijing government, however, now treats every person who sympathized with the students, or supported them financially, or even uttered any words of dissatisfaction with the government, as an enemy or a potential enemy. Telephone numbers were given in several big cities for people to report on others. All those reported on, no matter who the "reporter" was or what his or her motives, were regarded as suspects. The purpose was to make people live in constant fear.

"Knowing a crime but not reporting" is a crime. All the activities of students and citizens who participated in demonstrations and parades, donated money and food and clothing to students, and spoke to soldiers and blocked army vehicles were done in the open. Therefore, people must think about whether or not they should report these people to the government. If they do, perhaps they are also an object of someone else's report. When someone reports on another, he or she often finds that the other has reported on him or her. So, reporting on others may mean you reveal yourself—for if you were not there at the scene of the crime, how could you know what happened?

"Spreading rumors" is another crime. During the forty-odd days, almost everyone was passing information about possible moves by the government and the army. So many people might qualify as guilty of this crime.

The government cultivated this situation. During the first few days of arrests, it publicized a "criminal who spread rumors." This person was Xiao Bin, who used to be a worker in Dalian and later possibly a salesperson. The Beijing government made a recording of a scene from an American TV program in which the forty-two-year-old Xiao Bin related with great excitement what he had witnessed to the American journalist and the people around him. The Beijing government accused him of creating rumors and stirring up resentment. He said: "I saw with my own eyes that army vehicles ran over people and killed them. There were even more people who were shot to death! People were crushed to a pulp under tanks and armored vehicles. The soldiers also shot them with guns, beat them with clubs. After people were knocked out, the soldiers shot them. Those who did not die from one shot were given additional shots. Some were even killed with bayonets!" Xiao Bin raised two fingers, saying: "By now more than twenty thousand people have been killed! It was too cruel! There was never anything like it before! Many people are trying to think of a way out. If they [the soldiers] come out, they will be killed one by one!"

According to an official Chinese report, two young women in Dalian recognized his face after watching TV and reported him to the police. So he was arrested. First on TV in Dalian, then on the central TV station, these two women (after careful preparation), accused Xiao Bin and "exposed" his "crime." About a month later, the *People's Daily* reported: "Xiao Bin, who has committed counterrevolutionary propaganda crimes, has been sentenced to ten years' imprisonment, plus three years of deprivation of political rights." Apart from the above-mentioned crime, the paper also said: "After Xiao Bin returned to Dalian, he stirred up the masses to oppose the Communist Party of China and the people's government. He rumored that 'more than a thousand workers in Beijing jointly submitted their resignations from the Communist Party'; 'what the radio and TV advocate is all false'; and called people in Dalian 'all cowards, useless, slaves!' "

Judging by stories from reporters from Hong Kong and Taiwan, and from many other eyewitnesses, what Xiao Bin said about the massacre was largely true. (Only the number twenty thousand dead is questionable.) His report that civilians were going to kill soldiers was not rumor either, for it was proved by the actions of people in Beijing before he was sentenced.

But those who wish to resign from the Communist Party, are likely to far exceed a thousand. His opinion of the people of Dalian is not baseless. This is a city with a population of several million. It has many institutions of higher education, and it is also an industrial center. Over the years, it has been quiet, and did not participate in several of the national student movements and demonstrations. This time, very few students there took action. Nevertheless, when the *People's Daily* said that "Xiao Bin admitted in court that what he said was all rumors," it was true. We have also seen Xiao Bin admitting his crime to the police on TV. Chinese people could all understand that Xiao Bin's admission was against his will, for this is sometimes the only choice people can make under such circumstances. Should Xiao Bin have insisted that what he said was all true, and not rumors, he might have gotten a life sentence or even death.

This report was similar to the report of the arrest of Zhou Fengsuo, a student leader in Beijing, who was turned in by his own sister and brother-in-law. The government was apparently trying to get a message across to the people: Betray anyone without any fear or other consideration. This was the message of terrorism: Don't think you can hide your crime. Don't think your hideout is safe. Those who know you or those who don't know you can report on you. Give yourself up!

Deng and his clique even broke some of the basic principles and policies of the Mao period. For instance, in all political movements since the 1950s, Mao's principle of "we should not kill anyone, and do not arrest people in general," was observed. In 1957, even though Mao labeled more than a million people "rightists who are against the Party and socialism," most were not sentenced or imprisoned. Even his political enemies did not lose their personal freedom until the Cultural Revolution. During the case of opposing "the Hu Feng Clique" and the antireactionaries movement in the 1950s, when more people were arrested, very few were executed. When Mao said, "Unite all the people who can be united" and "Reduce the scope of attack," this might have had a hypocritical side; but in reality, Mao rarely killed ordinary people. Instead, he always attacked intellectuals and opposition within the Party. He even divided rightists into six categories and treated each differently.

This time, the Gang of the Old violated all the old rules—even those of the Mao period—expanding the attack to its largest possible extent, while reducing its own base of support to a very small area. At first, there was the slaughter in Beijing, followed by arrests throughout China, quick sentences, and quick executions. They even abandoned what Mao had always considered wise policy: "Divide the enemy camp to the greatest possible extent, so that real enemies will be separated out and isolated."

By now, according to relatively reliable calculations, in the Beijing area alone, there have been more than ten thousand arrests; and there have been a hundred and twenty thousand arrests throughout China. In Qingdao, a medium-sized city, more than two thousand people reportedly were arrested a few days after the massacre of June 4. The government wants not only those who got deeply involved with the Democracy movement and had a strong impact on students and civilians, such as political scientist Yan Jiaqi and historian Bao Zunxin, but also those who did not participate in political movements, such as literary theorist Liu Zaifu and aesthetician Li Zehou. Some only signed their names to an open letter, and some only asked others to sign for them. But they were still considered criminals.

The Gang of the Old and those officials and intellectuals who are dependent on them deeply resent the fact that several movements since 1981 against "bourgeois liberalization" and "spiritual contamination" did not succeed, and that their opponents became stronger and more influential in the cultural and academic fields. When Deng attributed the Democracy movement to the irresolute struggles against "bourgeois liberalization," he just provided an excuse for the thorough revenge under way. All those who had their own ideas and did not agree with traditional dogmas; all those who made some discoveries on their own; all those who were dissatisfied with the corruption of the Party and were brave enough to expose it; and all those who wanted to reform the political system since 1979 in the media, academia, the arts, and education became targets of attack. Some of them had been on the blacklist in the past, but were spared punishment. Some even had some influence on the national or provincial levels. But more often people have written only one or two essays or poems, or spoken at some meetings. Now, all these people have become objects of punishment.

All over China, everyone is worried about what will happen to them. All over the country, it is a scene of withered trees and fallen leaves in the cultural and ideological worlds. The expanded freedom of the press, hard-won by the journalists' efforts, has disappeared. Many journals and newspapers have been closed down. There are no more scholarly conferences. The Fifth Chinese Writers' Conference, originally planned for May, has been postponed indefinitely, for many of the most qualified writers are either in prison or in exile. Many literary and academic journals have stopped publication, because the present standards of censorship disqualify most of the works—and their authors are either arrested or in exile, or dare not produce or send in any new works. The distribution of news has again returned to the state of the 1970s—only one voice.

There is even book-burning. Aside from pornographic books, many famous Chinese and foreign authors have been banned. More than a thousand titles on Western thought translated from other languages have been labeled "forbidden books."

Almost all the major streets in Beijing are guarded by armed soldiers. In all cities, uniformed and plainclothes police are arresting people every day. Coastal cities and ports are even more heavily guarded so that nobody can escape from China. People are called on to expose "elements of rebellion." Reward money in tantalizing amounts is used to induce people to assist in arrests. The highest award money reaches 100,000 yuan ($25,000—about as much as an ordinary person on the mainland would earn in a hundred years' time).

Everywhere, executions of elements for "rebellion" are going on. According to a member of the Standing Committee of the Politburo in charge of propaganda, from now on all executions will be conducted in secret, in order not to stimulate foreign public opinion. The Chinese no longer dare to have contact with foreigners—they go out of their way to avoid them. Since more and more telephone conversations are being listened to, people no longer talk freely on the phone.

Censorship of letters has risen, especially letters to and from foreign countries. Chinese TV stations intentionally exaggerate this. For instance, one day a news item featured a special report of how letters from overseas are examined, and told Chinese viewers, that on that particular day, there were more than 4,500 documents of counterrevolutionary propaganda from other countries. It warned Chinese that they must hand in any letter of this nature to the authorities.

In order to prise information from those arrested, many of them were cruelly tortured. Four months after the June 4 massacre, a French reporter went to a village near the Summer Palace in the northwest suburbs of Beijing, where there is a school for juvenile delinquents. The villagers told him that the school had been taken over by the martial-law troops and was used to jail political prisoners. The villagers couldn't get to sleep at night for the terrible screams coming from behind the high walls of the school.

As under Mao Zedong and Lin Biao, politics is accentuated in the propaganda and practice of the Communist Party. Rock music is forbidden. Fashion models' performances on stage are canceled. Political standards become the primary standards for publications as well as performances. Pop music begins to be rejected, replaced by songs like "Party, my dear Party! You are my dearest mother!" At the beginning of the Cultural Revolution, Mao stopped the enrollment of all college students. Later, he allowed only students in science and technology. Deng has done the same thing: this fall, the number of students to be enrolled will be cut by thirty thousand. Only eight hundred students will be enrolled in Beijing University, one-third of its usual enrollment. Most of the cuts are in the liberal arts. The government also announced that all freshmen must receive military training before they are allowed to do normal studies. And the treatment of students at Beijing University is especially severe—freshmen must receive a full year of military training before they are allowed to study. (Have the policymakers thought about whether the students might influence the soldiers more than the reverse during this one year?)

This persecution has a large element of vindictiveness in it. The young poet Ye Wenfu, who published his poems in 1980, had one entitled "General, You Must Not Do So!" It exposed the corruption and degeneration of high-ranking army officers. Most of the generals hated him; the Cultural Department of the General Political Department, plus representatives of conservatives in cultural circles, began to persecute Ye Wenfu. This lasted for over five years. Ye could no longer publish his work. His working conditions and standard of living also worsened. Only after 1985 was he allowed to leave the army and participate in the normal creative activities of the Hubei Writers' Association. After the June 4 massacre, Ye was again targeted for persecution. He was arrested by Beijing soldiers and beaten severely many times. Because he could no longer bear the physical and the spiritual pain, he made several suicide attempts. But he was stopped by the guards. Now, Ye is exceptionally weak, and even if he is released, he may not survive long.

FOOLISH DECEIT

When the Gang of the Old decided to slaughter people, they forgot to plan one thing: how to explain to the world what happened. Once again, they probably lived in their memory of a time when all the doors were closed. TV and telecommunications technology were then not advanced in China. Perhaps they had forgotten that even now, more than a thousand foreign reporters are working in Beijing. When they began to lie, they forgot the tremendous political changes that have taken place in China and in the world over the past twenty years; they forgot that the lies Mao had used many times would not be very effective now.

What they remembered was the propaganda script for the 1956 revolution in Hungary. At that time it was called the "Hungarian Counterrevolutionary Rebellion." Good; this one too would be called a "counterrevolutionary rebellion"! According to Zhang Gong, director of the Political Department of the Beijing troops, during the process of quelling the "rebellion," the army "never fired one shot at the people." Another member of the same troops, Li Ziyun, very elaborately explained the whole process of how the troops progressed, saying that they were blocked by the people and were attacked by thugs until they could "no longer tolerate it; they shot into the sky with restraint, as warning. But they never shot at the masses, much less at the old and the children."

But somebody else wrote the script for Yuan Mu, spokesman for the State Council, using a different set of facts. A few words gave the story away. He said, During the quelling of this counterrevolutionary rebellion, a few thousand officers and soldiers of the People's Army were wounded. Civilian casualties were two thousand. Three hundred were killed. (Since it is hard to tell how to distribute the numbers of dead among rebels and those who quelled the rebellion, the numbers are glossed over.) Only twenty-three students were killed. (He was trying to put the number as low as possible, in order to avoid stimulating hatred toward the government.)

This is like a fairy tale: The fully armed soldiers with their tanks and armored vehicles, against unarmed students and civilians. How could the soldiers get killed at a rate several times more than the latter? Chen Xitong, mayor of Beijing, came out on stage to mend this oversight, saying there were more than three thousand nonmilitary people wounded, and more than two hundred people died, including thirty-six students.

Chen Xitong has always been very good at making up stories. Within seven days of the start of demonstrations by the Beijing students, he and Li Ximing, secretary of the Beijing Municipal Committee, made a report, according to the orders and needs of Deng Xiaoping, concluding that the students had started a counterrevolutionary rebellion. This time, though, Chen Xitong only told the last half of the story—how many soldiers were dragged off the armored vehicles by the civilians, how two soldiers were beaten to death, and even burned afterward. "The cruelty against the People's Liberation Army makes people's hair stand on end!" But, what about the first half of the story? Did the citizens of Beijing simply go crazy? If the soldiers had not shot people and run over people with tanks and armored vehicles, what followed would not have happened.

State-controlled TV and radio stations constantly and repeatedly broadcast the following scenes: rebels burning army vehicles; students throwing stones and bricks at the soldiers, tanks, and armored vehicles; and one soldier being hanged and burned by students.

135

A soldier named Cui Guozheng rendered outstanding service with his death. The deputy of the company commander said through a spokesman: Before Cui was killed, he was fleeing when three old ladies kneeled down in front of him, begging him not to kill more people. Cui shouted to them, asking them to get out of the way, because students were chasing him; and if he were captured, he would be killed. What the deputy of the company commander wanted to say is that he did not kill people—for three old ladies were right in front of him. But he did not mention why so many people were chasing him and why he was so scared. The reason is that he had just killed at least four civilians.

Cui Guozheng was recognized retroactively as a hero. In order to stress the importance and sacredness of his unfinished mission, TV and radio stations made special reports on how his sister joined the army in order to take up his unfinished work. This girl from Shandong Province has big eyes and thick eyebrows. Standing among male soldiers, and with submachine guns in front of her, she looks very serious and dignified. But it never occurs to her that both her brother and she herself have acted as tools of the Gang of the Old of the Communist Party—the brother killed civilians and the sister helped decorate the killer as a hero. Nor did she know that her brother's charred body was left hanging from a burned bus for three days, to serve the propaganda purposes of the Gang of the Old.

Of course, this is only a small part of the big lie that the Gang of the Old has had to fabricate. The rest of it is copied from Mao Zedong. The problem, however, is that this time, at least two hundred thousand students joined the "counterrevolutionary rebellion"—and that does not include the civilians who were blocking the armored vehicles and soldiers. Isn't it true that Mao liked say there were only "a small handful" of counterrevolutionaries? But now there were too many. So the Gang of the Old had to look for a "small handful of counterrevolutionaries" behind the masses of counterrevolutionary people.

Who were the "black hands" or "conspirators" behind this "premeditated, organized" rebellion? The first ones specified were Fang Lizhi and his wife Li Shuxian. Among Chinese intellectuals, Fang Lizhi was the earliest one to break openly with the Party. He was ousted from the Party in the most recent movement against "bourgeois liberalization." This couple also had some contacts with the students.

As the movement grew larger and larger, however, one couple like Fang and Li was not enough. What the Truth Department of the socialist government in George Orwell's *1984* did had to be done again. Zhao Ziyang himself became the "black hand." Fang Lizhi shrank to secondary importance. Only now a few Chinese would not be enough, decided the Gang of the Old; the conspiracy had to have a history and some international background.

Therefore, in Mayor Chen Xitong's speech, the title of the first part was, "There Has Been a Long History of Preparation and Premeditation of This Movement." The first sentence is, "All the political powers of the Western world have always wanted to make socialist countries, including China, give up the socialist road, and go on the capitalist road—this has been their basic policy for a long time." It goes on, "In our country, an extreme minority of people, who stubbornly persist in the bourgeois liberalization and engage in political conspiracies within and outside the Party, corresponded with this policy of the West. They have contacts in China and abroad, at all levels, and made preparations in ideology, public opinion, and organization, with the purpose of creating rebellion in China, overthrowing the leaders of the Communist Party, and sabotaging socialism."

This speech was given in early July. By the end of July, the responsibility of foreign countries had increased. A memorandum of the Central Committee of the Communist Party says, "The biggest international background of the counterrevolutionary rebellion is that the reactionary force of international capitalists have never stopped for a moment trying to effect a 'peaceful transformation' of China." "In the name of 'democracy' and 'human rights', they are selling the capitalist congress and multiparty system . . . and proposing that they should encourage the socialist countries' tendency toward liberalism. . . ."

But the question arises: Did "international capitalism" invade China with warships and cannons, or was it invited into China by Deng Xiaoping? Since it is so hideous and disgusting, why was Deng, afraid that it was arriving too slowly and too little, opening so many special economic zones? If he had known this earlier, he should have agreed with Chen Yun and Deng Liqun and thrown away both the special economic zones and the open-door policy. In addition, since Deng Xiaoping has now realized the evil of this influence, why does he still keep saying that reform and the open-door policy will remain unchanged?

There is no satisfactory answer for Deng to proclaim. So Zhao Ziyang will be accused of collaborating with international, primarily American, capitalist forces. Perhaps before long, we shall see that the CIA has also played a part in the Democracy movement. We don't see it now; instead, we see the Voice of America. Never mind, Mayor Chen Xitong already has unearthed important criminal evidence. "Some people in America, England, and Hong Kong donated a million US dollars and dozens of millions of Hong Kong dollars. Part of this money was used in activities to sabotage martial law. Every person who participated in building roadblocks and who stopped troops from coming in was given an award of thirty yuan. Meanwhile, they also promised high awards to rebels, asking them to burn military vehicles—three thousand yuan for burning one vehicle, several thousand for capturing or killing one soldier." Mayor Chen left out the names of those who gave the money. This way, Chinese readers could, based on past experience, guess that it might be the CIA, or secret agents in Taiwan. But what the mayor can never tell readers in mainland China is that the donations were made by Chinese students who are studying abroad, overseas Chinese, and some American citizens. He also left out the source of the Hong Kong dollars.

To paint Zhao Ziyang as the "black hand" behind this movement was a bit harder than smearing Fang Lizhi. They had to reverse the logic of the events of the past few years. In order to bring about reform, Zhao needed a group of middle-aged and young intellectuals, a talented "brain trust." They formed institutions like the Research Institute for Reform of the Economic System and the Research Institute for Reform of the Political System. They naturally had contacts with intellectuals and students in Beijing's cultural and academic circles. Now this sequence had to be reversed. All their activities and relationships, we now learn, were aimed solely at

139

helping Zhao Ziyang realize his conspiracy against the Party and his instigation of "counterrevolutionary rebellion." Naturally, all Zhao's assistants had to be arrested.

The Gang of the Old could not produce any theory, ideology, or method of propaganda different from the ones used in former times. Every harsh step was "due to the need for revolution"; everyone had to "fear neither hardship nor death"; "we must limit and reduce personal freedom in order to prevent imperialist invasion and cultural infiltration." In their theory, humanism belongs to the bourgeoisie, and asceticism is the revolutionary virtue everyone should have. Since they could find no evidence or theory to support their actions, they could only play the old tunes and tell the old lies. They could only use power to force people to "show their attitude" against their will.

But the Gang of the Old is still under the illusion that the Chinese are the same as they were in the 1960s, easy to fool. In a recent speech, Deng Xiaoping mentioned many times that the Party should "win the trust of the people." In order to "keep the people satisfied, we must do a few good things." First among them is to penalize some Party officials for their economic crimes, in order to convince people that the Gang of the Old is indeed against corruption.

In any small town, people could see the most influential, comfortable, and profitable positions all occupied by children of leaders. When workers and ordinary office clerks could not find housing after years of waiting, some officials could obtain new apartments or houses without using them. They could even rent or sell them to make a profit. In many towns and cities, children of officials could rape women without being punished by law. Officials used their power or connections to cover up for criminals, so they would not be punished. Or they would persecute those who dared to expose their criminal activities, so that they would not be rehabilitated for a long time. Economic crimes and illegal racketeering could be seen in almost all towns and cities. Since the early 1980s, it has been widely known throughout China that children of high-ranking officials have bank accounts in other countries. They are said to have kept money from the foreign trade that they monopolized, so that they could use it when needed. In counties that could survive only on government subsidies, officials used public funds to buy imported cars, or embezzled funds set aside for disaster relief to build office buildings and private apartments.

So, starting in July, there have been more and more reports in the official newspapers about penalizing corrupt officials. It almost seemed as if the Communist Party was going to do something "real" this time. But the Chinese rank-and-file want to see if the sons and daughters of high-ranking officials will be penalized. "What happens to Deng's son and son-in-law?" "What happens to Wang Zhen's son?" "And where are the three sons of Bo Yibo?" "You will really dare to touch Peng Zhen's son and daughter?" They also want to see how the Gang of the Old deal with the big bank accounts of the high-ranking officials and their children.

Of course, if what they see first is that Zhao Ziyang's sons are punished, they will turn away, laughing, not wanting to go on watching this farce any more. For it is the usual practice to punish the children of a disgraced official. Nowadays, even ordinary urban dwellers understand this: fighting corruption is just an empty word without thoroughly reforming the present political system. How many large-scale anticorruption campaigns were conducted during Mao's times? What did they ultimately achieve? Nothing. The reason is simple: Mao Zedong never used the political system or legal restraints to limit the power of officials and subject them to the effective supervision; instead he depended on initiating frequent campaigns against corruption to punish guilty officials. But without a free press, even though the criminal activities of such officials were exposed, they were often handled in secret and treated leniently. Ordinary people and reporters had no legal support in their struggle against corruption.

Conversely, the connections formed since 1949 among officials have effectively helped them protect one another from being punished by law. So they have become "special citizens" whose conduct was above the law.

NO LONGER THE SAME PEOPLE

Since 1986, the leaders of the Communist Party have always been worried as important festivals and anniversaries approached, afraid that students would take to the streets and demonstrate. So every May 1, International Labor Day; every October 1, National Day; every May 4, Youth Day (and the anniversary of the democracy movement of 1919); even every September 18, the anniversary of the Japanese invasion of three provinces in the Northeast, Party leaders have been exceptionally cautious. This is ironic, because in the forty years since 1949, the Chinese Communist Party would organize people to celebrate the first three festivals and anniversaries, and encourage people to parade or have gatherings to show how grateful and loyal they were to the Party. But not now. This October

1 was a very unusual National Day. Martial law in Beijing still could not be canceled; army troops still could not leave, for the Gang of the Old were afraid that the residents and students of Beijing would take to the streets again to express their anger and hatred.

The Gang of the Old and its followers are always quick to protect their security. Hated by the people of Beijing, Li Ximing, secretary of the Municipal Committee of Beijing, and Mayor Chen Xitong added guards to their residences. Members of the Gang of the Old and their children no longer dare ride in the Mercedes-Benzes that they used to show off in the streets. They would rather use Japanese cars, for fear of bomb attacks or being shot by snipers. The Gang of the Old has already discovered that the barrel of the gun did not give them the kind of authority that they had imagined. Their fear is not without foundation.

Soldiers who are carrying out martial law dare not walk in the streets alone. They are afraid of being murdered when they walk in dark alleys. Guards in the streets are occasionally shot by snipers. Therefore, two soldiers often stand back to back together in order to prevent attack from all possible directions.

The journalists in Beijing were very brave during the Democracy movement. Therefore, the Gang of the Old decided long ago that they would be major targets of attack. After June 5, many editors and reporters still dared to express resistance. The *People's Daily* published a notice saying that due to a lack of paper, the paper would have only four pages, instead of the usual eight. Meanwhile, it communicated information to people in a roundabout way. For instance, it carried a report about South Korea where people were trying to discover the architect of the Kwangju massacre—implying that this is an action

143

the Chinese will have to take. The military reorganized the editorial boards of all newspapers and forced all members to come to work. But editors and reporters slowed down, so that the main pages of the papers had to be filled with news from the official Xinhua News Agency.

Since the Mao period, it has been a standard practice during every political movement for the Central Committee to select, from among intellectuals and representatives of the democratic parties, some to express their support for the "wise decisions" of the Central Committee and to criticize those being attacked. In the campaign against "bourgeois liberalization," few wanted to speak up. This time, the Central Committee must have tried hard to find people who would show their support. So far, the response has been extraordinarily cold. At a forum of "democratic parties" and people with no party affiliations, of the eleven people that spoke, only five positively supported the "quelling" of the "counterrevolutionary rebellion." The others talked about unrelated subjects.

At the Eighth Conference of the Standing Committee of the National People's Congress, which had been postponed and had had its topic changed completely, the Central Committee wanted to pass legislation to prevent any future demonstrations in Beijing or elsewhere in China. What the Gang of the Old did not expect was that more than one member of the Standing Committee opposed discussion and passing of this legislation. Among them were not only Tao Dayong, a democratic personage, but also Wang Wei, former vice-minister of the Ministry of Health. Many other members held the same view.

Those who refuse to attend such meetings, and refuse to comply with the wishes of the Gang of the Old when they do speak, apparently disagree with Deng's massacre. Under such great pressure, it must take tremendous courage to resist even that passively.

When ordinary citizens of Beijing could not go into the streets to shout slogans, they thought of other ways to release their anger. Since all the cities have set up special telephone lines for people to report on the "rebels," people would often pick up the phone and report on themselves:

> I realize that I have committed the crime of supporting the counterrevolutionary rebellion. The crime should be punished by death. I am asking the government to punish me. On such and such a date, I took part in the student demonstrations and shouted slogans of "Down with Li Peng!" On such and such a date, I went to Tiananmen Square and gave students bread.

There were many such phone calls. Some callers not only reported on themselves, but also on others, listing dozens or even hundreds of names of people in the workplace, from ordinary staff to cadres. These calls left the soldiers perplexed. How could they arrest so many "counterrevolutionary rebels"? Those who made such phone calls did not do this just for fun; they were blocking the line so that real informers could not get through.

Many Chinese students were studying abroad, in America, Europe, and Australia; most went all out for the Democracy movement, raising funds to support students inside China. They learned the latest developments by calling relatives and friends in China, then spread the news to gain the support of international public opinion.

After June 4, they no longer called their families or friends, for it would bring them trouble. Instead, they collected the numbers of fax machines in China, and sent and received information about the suppression that took place. They also used various channels to send videotapes that recorded the brutal massacre. A group of Chinese reporters traveling in America also published a *Freedom of the Press Herald* and sent it to China. Some students abroad specialized in sabotaging the hot-lines for telling on people in China.

Many active young people have gone underground. Underground political organizations have sprung up in many parts of China. They conduct extensive political-enlightenment work and publish underground pamphlets and newsletters. Many student leaders, intellectuals, and entrepreneurs have fled to other countries. A Democratic China Front that aims at demanding democracy for China and opposing the June 4 massacre was formally announced in Paris in September.

All college students and graduates are forced to "study" Deng's speech and other such documents. All those who work in government institutions and social organizations have to spend two hours each day "studying" such documents, and furthermore, have to speak about in what ways they have enhanced their understanding of this "counterrevolutionary rebellion" and corrected their mistaken conceptions. This is "unifying the thought"—a method used from the fifties up to the Cultural Revolution. In the fifties, people did it of their own free will, so it was relatively effective. But now, what kind of result will it have if people are forced to study the "instructions" of the executioners they hate, and criticize relatives and friends who have been killed or arrested? During such "study," people are not allowed to keep silent; they have to say something. But in their hearts they are cursing the Gang of the Old.

Unable to bear the oppression, students at Beijing University toward the end of July found their own way to release their anger and frustration. More than two hundred students on campus began to beat their bowls and plates with spoons and chopsticks, while singing in a distorted voice a song the Party likes to hear: "Without the Communist Party, There Would Be No New China."

Nor is it possible for the Chinese government to keep the truth of the June 4 massacre and the arrests throughout the country from the people for too long. Since about 1975, the loss of trust in the official propaganda, has made information by word of mouth the main channel of political news in China. Its efficiency and accuracy is often amazing.

With the economic reforms, word-of-mouth political news has had new advantages. For the Chinese people have drastically changed their lifestyle. Peasants who lived in one place for generations and never entered the nearest town now travel all over the country, engage in commerce, and deal with modern communications, greatly widening their horizons. News consequently now spreads relatively rapidly to the countryside. Curiosity about both domestic and international affairs has also been piqued; many peasants own transistor radios. Tired of the stereotyped formulas of official broadcasts, they turn to Chinese-language broadcasts from overseas to learn about what's going on in China. The Voice of America, the British Broadcasting Company, and radio stations from Australia, West Germany, Japan, and Taiwan are also gaining more and more listeners.

With the opening to the outside world, the first influence of the West was to expose the false propaganda of the Chinese Communist Party about the economic crises, poverty, crime, and strikes of the West. When the Chinese who have lived in poverty for so long saw the prosperity of most people in Western countries, they started to doubt or even abandon the ideology of Mao Zedong and their trust in the Chinese socialist system. Today, the pursuit of material comfort and the egoism of the West are gradually replacing the asceticism and altruism advocated by Mao Zedong. The works of Western thinkers mainly affected intellectuals and college students, but when Deng Xiaoping refused to reform the political system and opposed "liberalism," it only intensified their infatuation with the West.

Nor is this movement confined to urban areas. Since the mid-1980s, peasants have engaged in violent resistance to paying taxes and refused to hand in their grain. During the 1989 harvest, 126 officials and policemen sent to force farmers to sell or hand in their grain were killed or wounded in the Wuhan area. Only when you understand to what extent the farmers were exploited can you begin to realize why they would use such cruel methods against the grain collectors.

In 1988, the following incident took place in Henan Province. In July, Jin Changfu, Party secretary of Chenya district of this Minquan County, heard that a peasant, Cai Fawang, sixty-three, had refused to hand in his grain. Last year, the grain production of most districts in Minquan County had dropped by 49 percent. Cai Fawang's family only had some 700 jin (350 kilograms), only one-quarter of what they used to produce. But they were asked to hand in 400 jin. If they did, the whole family would starve.

The Party secretary sent a district official with five policemen to arrest him. The old peasant was forced into the car and beaten severely. When he arrived at the government offices, the official and the police continued to beat him. He was wounded in eighteen places all over his body (head, back, arms, testes, legs, and ears, which were cut open) and hanged himself that night in front of the police station.

Cai's death shook the counties around Minquan. Farmers surrounded the district offices and shouted and called names. Cai's family took the corpse to Jin Changfu's house, in the district government compound, saying they would not rest until they found the killer. It was summer. The weather was hot and the corpse began to stink. County officials tried to mediate several times, but were turned away. They also attempted to bury the corpse, but failed. The corpse of Cai rested in the government compound for 260 days, protected by the district people. Meanwhile, due to the farmers' resistance, no grain was collected. But the killer was never arrested.

During the famine of 1960, more than 7 million people, most of whom were peasants, starved to death in Henan. At that time, it was rare for peasants to oppose the county government to protect their own rights. But now in China the peasants have awakened, and are brave enough to stand up against the dictatorship and protect their own rights.

In 1987, there was a farmers' rebellion in Cangshan County, Shandong Province. It was not caused by politics, but the peasants' dissatisfaction with the Communist Party should not be underestimated. The previous year, the county government had encouraged peasants to expand the areas for growing scallions, and promised to arrange for collection and sales, at good rates. So the peasants did as they were told and harvested a bumper crop of scallions. But when they sent the tens of thousands of jin of scallions to the county seat, the government and the state-run commercial department were not prepared to sell it to the outside. Therefore, they bought only a small amount, on the pretext that there was limited capacity for refrigeration. Furthermore, according to custom, those peasants who had special relations with the government were treated favorably, which caused strong resentment.

By now, traders had come from other parts of China, willing to buy some of the scallions. And the peasants were of course willing to sell at a fair price. But the government officials thought that traders from outside must not get a bargain, so they decided to impose heavy taxes. As a result, the traders left in dissatisfaction.

Now there were already several million jin of scallions in the county, beginning to rot. When the peasants saw the fruit of their labor turn into nothing, and realized that the county officials never had their interest at heart at all, the fury and resentment gathered over many years erupted. Peasants used wheelbarrows, donkey carts, and shoulder poles to carry the rotting scallions inside the courtyard of the county government compound and dump them there. They smashed the doors and windows of the offices and office equipment, even broke open the safe and burned files and other documents. The peasants' could not recoup their loss; all they could do was protest and release their hatred and fury.

The county government and county committee naturally

thought this was a rebellion. So they used police and soldiers and arrested more than five hundred people. Then they tried to find out who started this to punish this person as a counter-revolutionary rebel. While in custody, five peasants committed suicide. The news spread all over the county. Tens of thousands of farmers rushed into the county government compound, attempting to encircle the county committee and rescue the other peasants being held in custody. The news reached Beijing. The central government hurried to send someone to this county, and stripped the head of the county of his title in order to appease the peasants and stop the rebellion.

About a year later, at the end of 1988, spontaneous protests took place on the city level. On December 24, about four months before the student movement in Beijing, more than two thousand people paraded for two days, in the streets of Yueyang City, Hunan Province, protesting corruption in the Party, and the dismissal of Vice-Mayor Yin Zhenggao by conservatives and corrupt officials. Yin Zhenggao was a middle-aged intellectual and an honest official. He was also sympathetic to people's pain and hardship.

People in Yueyang City saw in him hope for reform, and they called him the "Gorbachev of Yueyang City." He had made outstanding contributions in reforming the city's politics and economy after he was elected vice-mayor. But he kept exposing the illegal activities of officials at various levels who used their power for personal ends, publicizing this campaign, and eventually exposing the mayor's corruption and embezzling, so those people ganged up and attacked him, and finally dismissed him from his position.

His dismissal caused tremendous turmoil. People shouted,

"Oppose corruption! We want clean government!" "Support justice! Support reform, oppose regression!" "Give us back our mayor Yin!"

Because Yin's achievements were widely known and the demonstration in Yueyang City was the first spontaneous one since the student movement in 1986, it drew the whole country's attention, although this demonstration was never reported by the media—only by word of mouth. While the event was happening, many reporters were drawn to Yueyang. They tried hard to publicize this event, without success. But not one story or photograph about this was published. It was not until this January that a long report on the event was published in a literary journal.

Looking at the future of China's Democracy movement, it is hard to avoid some unfavorable facts. The Chinese Communist Party has done great damage to China's economy and culture. About one-quarter of China's population lives in poverty. About 200 million people are illiterate. The level of education cannot be compared with that in the Soviet Union and Eastern European countries. There is no active tradition of democracy or enlightenment in China. The factions that have always existed in China's political life will undoubtedly continue to complicate change.

The history of the Cultural Revolution and aspects of the Democracy movement show that once people have acquired some democratic rights and freedom, the factional struggles among various interest groups can take precedence over the struggle against common enemies. The democratic fighters lacked the habits of democratic life. A few student leaders overestimated their own strength and influence, and did not respect—and even put down and opposed—others. These tendencies, as well as the struggle for personal fame and power, all caused great damage to the movement. They created conflicts in the movement and provided enemies with opportunities to attack. The excessively radical mood expressed by the students in the spring of 1989 reminded people of the "leftist" tendencies that were often evident during revolutionary movements in the past twenty years in China.

Nevertheless, people's democracy movements also have unique advantages. The difference between China and some countries of the Eastern bloc is that China has gone through the Cultural Revolution. The unquestioned authority of the Communist Party, its ideology, and its organization have been greatly reduced if not destroyed. As a result, the Chinese Party's control over the people has become much looser. The Cultural Revolution also created a generation of young people with a rebellious spirit, who are familiar with what is happening at the lowest levels of society. Many of them have already become established in the political, economic, and cultural circles. Compared with Romania, North Korea, and Burma, which have been closed to the outside for a long time, China has the advantage of having ten years of economic reform and opening to the outside world. The presence of millions of overseas Chinese in Hong Kong and Taiwan is also an advantage these other countries do not have. The patriotic overseas Chinese have just begun to exert their influence on the mainland. And although their potential is just beginning to be released, it has already had a tremendous impact.

For the cause of democratization in China, the greatest shortcoming is the lack of an organized political power. The Chinese people have no political organizations of their own, nor have they any publications of their own—but still they managed to break through all kinds of bans and military interceptions. Millions of people marched in the streets of Beijing in perfect order. And in hundreds of smaller cities, people also held spontaneous demonstrations. Tens of millions of people marched in various cities and towns in China, with but a single demand: democracy. They marched regardless of the strenuous opposition of the official organizations—Party and youth-league committees, local governments, trade unions, student associations—and regardless of the possible acts of revenge they would face, the loss of of bonuses, of jobs, of status. The demonstrations of 1986 and 1987 took place in only a dozen big cities, and only students participated; but in the spring of 1989, only two years later, more than two hundred cities were involved. If we extrapolate this rate of change in the political situation, this rate of development in popular political awareness, we can predict major changes ahead, and we cannot be far wrong.

The next wave of China's movement toward democracy will arrive when its social crises, especially its financial crisis, come to a head.

ECONOMIC CRISIS AND REGRESSION

Deng started his economic reform when China's economy was facing collapse at the late 1970s. Ten years later, Deng, together with the Gang of the Old, again faces economic collapse. Since October 1988, the Beijing government has adopted a series of urgent measures to tighten its control over the economy. Since June 1989, the return to the old political system and economic policy will surely leave the officials in charge of economy at various levels, and the directors of state-run and collective-run factories, perplexed. For they are afraid of taking the political responsibility for capitalism. As for privately owned enterprises and private entrepreneurs, they were originally afraid of the "capitalist" label and of having their property confiscated, so they used most of their profits for consumption, and not to expand production. They are so frightened now that they would rather sell their businesses.

What Deng is most afraid of is that the flow of money, trade, and investments from other countries might stop. Even though the government claimed it was not afraid of economic sanctions, it has already reduced the price of certain products for export by 10 percent and raised the price of imports by 10 percent, in order to induce foreign traders to do business with China. China already has a huge deficit. To enhance China's competitive power, concessions are needed. Once prices rise or fall it will be hard to change them, unless there is intense competition in the international market. So the budget deficit is certain to increase. Last year's deficit was 16 billion yuan (the official version was 7.8 billion yuan). This year, the deficit will reach 27 billion yuan.

In the past forty years, the so-called ownership by the people has in fact been ownership of more than 90 percent of the nation's wealth by the state. Chinese workers, for instance, are masters of the country in name only. In fact, they have no right to manage or administer any of the wealth owned by "the people." And officials at different levels who are in charge of this wealth take no responsibility for it. At least one-third of all the industrial enterprises built by workers, farmers, and intellectuals with blood and sweat are useless, lying there rusting away. Due to lack of energy and raw materials, about one-third of all the factories have to stop production. Those that can function are open only four or five days a week. Compared with factories in other countries, the Chinese factories are wasteful and produce little profit. Many of their products are not needed in the market. For instance, over thirty million tons of steel are in storage and cannot be sold; nonetheless, China has to import several million tons of steel each year.

The economic reform enabled some Chinese peasants and urban residents to increase their income and improve their living standards. But the reform was not thorough enough, so their income has been unstable. Since the mid-1980s, peasants and private entrepreneurs have had a harder and harder life. Only a few corporations run by the bureaucratic bourgeoisie and those who had connections with high-ranking officials have been able to make big profits and feel secure. But it is precisely because these people were enjoying special privileges that the common people were deeply dissatisfied with the new injustices brought about by the reform.

At the beginning of 1989, there were more than 2,000 private enterprises and household businesses, and 36 million people worked in such enterprises. They produced one-tenth of national retail sales. Industry profit rates in this sector also far exceeded those of state-run enterprises. But with the campaign against spiritual contamination since 1983, these entrepreneurs became more and more nervous. They have not dared to expand their production or deposit their profits in banks, for fear of revealing their wealth.

After the Beijing spring of 1989, private enterprises and industrialists went bankrupt in great numbers. According to the *China Daily*, in the first six months of 1989, private enterprises in China decreased by 15 percent. Peasants had to sell their produce to the state at low prices and buy materials from the state at high prices. This has become a national phenomenon. In addition, taxes are also driving farmers in many areas to desperation. This is why so many peasants give up farming and go to other parts of China. The rising inflation since 1985 has lowered the living standards of urban residents. Office clerks, workers, and teachers who depend on a fixed salary for a living have the hardest time.

On the other hand, the Chinese government could not do anything to appease the peasants. On the contrary, it had to irritate them. The government could not raise the price for collecting grain from peasants. And it dare not raise the prices of food and cooking oil being sold to the peasants. Now peasants have to sell their grain at one-third or one-fifth of the market price to the government. Peasants, of course, are unwilling to do this. Consequently, in recent years, collecting grain in the country has been like fighting a war. Party officials lead the way, followed by police. The peasants are vigilant. In some places, every time the grain collecting season comes, the village is organized, with someone standing guard. As soon as officials are spotted, the guard will whistle. All the villagers then bolt their doors and escape to the fields. This is reminiscent of what farmers did during the Anti-Japanese War, under the leadership of the Communist Party. The familiar warning "Japanese devils are coming into the village!" was used again when troops entered Beijing in 1989.

What has irritated the peasants even more is that the government could not pay them cash for grain and other agricultural products last fall. So it gave them blank receipts. One old peasant drove his ox-cart to town early in the morning, to sell grain to the government. However, the government did not pay him cash, so he came back home empty-handed. With nothing but a useless receipt in his hand, he cried all the way. He had intended to use the money to buy some necessities for his family. But what store would accept a receipt?

The grain harvest in the summer of 1989 was fairly good. But the government could not pay even half of the money to buy the grain. This time, government officials decided they would not use blank receipts. Instead, they decided to pay with state bonds. As a result, although peasants had not cashed the blank checks from last year, they now had to "lend" half of their agricultural products to the country and could not expect any return for several years. But since in the last year alone the government printed at least 200 billion yuan, how could it have no money to pay the peasants? The reason is that people are now burying their money, willing even to bear the brunt of inflation. They do not trust the government. Last year, when the prices were rising rapidly, even those in Shanghai, who had the most faith in the Party, took their money out of the bank. Official as well as private traders stored tremendous amounts of cash, to be able to bribe corrupt officials and evade taxes. They did not keep money in the bank, creating a situation where one household would often have several hundred thousand yuan in its own safe.

The one mint in Beijing could not meet the demand, so another one was built recently, but still the demand could not be met. Every yuan that has already been issued corresponds to one yuan's worth of commodity. In normal times, the country should produce seven yuans worth of commodities for every yuan that is issued as currency. The inflation rate for last year was 40 percent. Zhang Wuchang, a Hong Kong economist, predicted after the June 4 massacre that before long the inflation rate on the mainland would reach three digits.

In short, all the problems, whether the Chinese people yet understand them fully or not, including their increasingly unpleasant moods, are now reflected in the currency. They last associated inflation with the collapse of the Kuomintang, and now they keep asking, Is the Communist Party also going to collapse soon?

It is true that the Kuomintang government's rule during 1948–1949 left people anxious about their security and caused prices to rise rapidly. But all that happened when a civil war was going on and the troops of the Communist Party already had overwhelming superiority. The cities controlled by the Kuomintang were all encircled by the People's Liberation Army. The peasants' sources of staples and other food were already cut off. Students and workers were organized by the Party to oppose the Kuomintang government. The government had lost control of the mass media, which was spreading all kinds of ideas that were destructive to the stability of its rule. All these factors, as well as the activities of various democratic parties against the Kuomintang, played important roles in accelerating the social crisis.

The same situation does not exist on the mainland today. Nevertheless, one thing is similar. That is, the Kuomintang government was unable to stop hoarding and speculation by bureaucrats and businessmen; the Communist Party also is unable to stop economic crime and the corruption of bureaucrats and their children. Since most of the economy of China is controlled by the government, it should be able to control it much better than the Kuomintang did. But all the signs indicate that Deng Xiaoping and the Gang of the Old have much less inclination to solve these problems than they displayed in the massacre of students and civilians in Beijing in June. In fact, they do not acknowledge the problems.

Slowdowns rather than strikes were popular forms of resistance, during the Anti-Japanese War. During the Cultural Revolution, the fact that workers showed up for work but did not produce anything irritated the Gang of Four, but there was nothing they could do about it. Since the mid-1980s, slowdowns to signal worker dissatisfaction have again become common. One rubber products factory in Beijing maintained normal production during the Cultural Revolution. The one-hundred-odd workers managed to produce more than a million yuan in profit. In the 1980s, however, the factory began to operate at a loss. The reason was that the first thing every director assigned to this factory did was to raise his own salary, assign friends to important positions, and then go to scenic spots all over China, ostensibly for business. One director even changed the production process and equipment so that the quality of the products fell and costs rose. Workers saw all this and were very angry. But they had no power to correct it. So they expressed their dissatisfaction by slowdowns and even by knocking over the rubber containers. Stealing state property to protest against the present system and to improve low living standards is another popular method of opposition. In recent years, the scale of such sabotage has reached astounding proportions. According to incomplete statistics, the country's loss through this avenue alone amounted to millions of yuan.

What Deng Xiaoping does not understand is that even after he has repeatedly limited the freedom of the press, workers can

160

still see many social problems and injustices. When they find themselves unable to do anything about these problems, they will slow down, and sometimes even engage in sabotage as an outlet for their pent-up dissatisfaction. Deng thinks he has the answer to all accusations and dissatisfactions. That is, no matter what happens, "Our aim of doubling the gross national product has been achieved. The quadrupling is expected to take twenty years to complete. . . . After sixty-one years, it would be a tremendous achievement for a country with a population of 1.5 billion to achieve middle-level development."

The Chinese people, however, no longer have the patience to wait this long. Nor will the economic situation make Deng very complacent this year. According to the statistics of the Chinese Ministry of Finance, the industry run by the state did badly in the first six months of 1989. Profits decreased and costs increased in each month. The enterprises that were operating at a loss made up about 19 percent of all its existing enterprises. And the amount of loss increased rapidly—and was 1.22 times that of 1988. In the more important industrial areas, the problems were most serious. The income for the government was greatly reduced and expenditures rose. It was predicted that the government would have to make up the loss caused by price increases and that enterprises which were losing money would account for about 32.6 percent of the expenditure.

Since the government tightened controls over the economy in October 1988, it has created 10 million unemployed who now float all over the country. After the June 4 massacre, many projects with foreign investment were halted. Funds stopped coming in, which will cause more unemployment. In state-run enterprises, there were already 30 million potential unemployed workers. These people are not only a great burden on the economy, they are also causing increasing social instability.

Since the start of this summer, China has witnessed a series of natural disasters. It is already certain that the fall harvests of grain will be low, just like last year. Peasants have very little grain in their hands. Due to lack of trust in the government, urban dwellers are trying to store grain for themselves. In Shandong Province, some people bought more than 2,000 jin of wheat flour for each household. Even if each household buys only 100 jin of grain in excess, that would lead to a severe shortage of grain. This in turn would create greater fear, leading to larger amounts of buying in excess and hoarding of grain. Famine is possible in China within a few years.

Daily necessities are becoming more scarce. On the other hand, purchasing power remains strong. Along with the rise in inflation, there might be another big rise in prices. Especially after the June 4 massacre, such an increase will create greater dissatisfaction with the political system. Economic confusion continues to grow, and together with further increases in prices and a decrease in living standards, will prompt workers to take action. Strikes are becoming more widespread.

Meanwhile, 1992 is approaching. By then China has to pay back foreign debts—$23 billion out of its $40 billion in debt. At the same time, China will have to pay back more than 100 billion yuan worth of inflation-proof deposits. Yet the revenue for all of 1988 was less than 22 billion yuan, not nearly enough to pay off the debts in 1992. It was possible, before the June 4 massacre, to borrow money to pay off old debts. But now China will have a hard time getting foreign loans. In the tourist industry alone in 1989, China has lost more than $1 billion. And China's internal turmoil will continue to frighten off foreign tourists.

China is facing a major choice: Should it return to the planned economy, or should it engage in greater use of the market? The former is gaining the upper hand right now. In Shanghai, one-third or more of the enterprises run by townships and districts have been disbanded. Beijing is planning to follow suit. However, at least 36 million people are working in private enterprises or as individual entrepreneurs. It is not possible to regress to the situation of the Cultural Revolution, where daily necessities were rationed. What follows, however, will not be social instability, but possibly greater turmoil.

THE PARTY IS DISINTEGRATING

After Jiang Zemin, the new Party general secretary took office, his long essay entitled "On the Question of Party Construction" was published. He held that in order to consolidate the Party, "we must give full rein to the Party's unifying power, attraction, and fighting power." Chinese readers immediately translated this passage into their own language: What Jiang meant was "The Chinese Communist Party is disintegrating (no unifying power and fighting power) and is opposed by the absolute majority of the Chinese people; its members are no longer docile tools of the Party, but each goes his own way."

Relatively few people even in China have access to information about inner Party struggles, especially splits and conflicts within Party organizations in the localities and at lower levels. In many counties, struggles between reformers and prodemocracy and anticorruption forces and those who are against reform and democracy—within the county committees, between county committees and county governments, between the Standing Committee of the People's Congress and

163

the county courts, within the county courts, as well as between county committees and various economic and cultural organizations—have never stopped, and are now reaching a level of tension that could lead to an explosion.

The former seek to realize the rights the constitution offers people, and try to expose the mistakes of the latter, to subject them to public opinion and report them to the Central Committee. They seek to use the People's Congress or elections at Party conferences to oust the latter. Or they use legal procedures to penalize criminal activities. The regressive forces rely on the "protective umbrella" of higher officials and their connections to cover up their criminal activities or mistakes, and to cover for each other. They take advantage of their power to slander, persecute, or even murder those who are brave enough to expose their criminal activities.

After the economic reform was implemented in 1979, the market economy and open policy created even more opportunities for officials to use their power for private ends. In foreign trade alone, these people make shocking illegal profits from sales commissions provided by foreign businessmen. However, compared with other damage done to the country, this is negligible. Many of the foreign-trade projects were monopolized by children of high-ranking officials. Within a few years' time, China has produced a new bureaucratic bourgeois stratum. Compared with the old one—one of the "Three Great Mountains" (imperialism, feudalism, and bureaucratic bourgeoisie) of the Kuomintang—it is much more harmful, because the earlier bourgeoisie, had fewer assets at its disposal, and it had some fear for law and order as well as for public opinion. These new people control the power to trade or distribute the resources, funds, and products of the country, and they use it for their own advantage. Among them, some are officials and some are former officials. The latter appear as directors and managers, using their former connections to engage in illegal activities to sell and resell the state's resources, products and raw materials.

As long as a Party official has one protector higher up in the organization and close connections with the same-level or lower-level officials, he or she enjoys virtually absolute freedom, regardless of rank. They can cover for each other. They can illegally take possession of public wealth, and bully or persecute those they are dissatisfied with or those who oppose them, without being punished. Not only that, they can even expect to be promoted. This protection extends to children and other relatives.

The Party organization is aware of the severity of these problems. Chen Yun had said at the beginning of the 1980s, "The question of the moral condition of the Party is a vital question for the party in power." Yet people like Deng Xiaoping and Chen Yun had neither the will nor the intention to solve this problem. The campaign to rectify the Party between 1983 and 1985 was a complete failure. Corruption among officials became worse. The two ways to curb corruption—freedom of the press and construction of a system of law—were both stymied. Though the Party Disciplinary Commission's main task was to check on corruption among Party officials, it in fact protected more people who were corrupt than it punished. Furthermore, those punished were usually relative minor officials whose activities had less serious consequences, or the disciplinary committees of the Party at various levels focused on penalizing the reformers within the Party.

This is an irony of history: The Chinese Communist Party has never allowed the existence of other parties (real independent parties instead of its affiliates). However, during the long years of the one-party system, the Party has produced out of its own belly several factions. In a strict sense, the Chinese Communist Party is no longer one unified party. There have always been two opposing forces within the party. The major conflict is that between democracy and autocracy. Since 1979, the conflict has changed to wanting reform or opposing reform.

Proreform forces have been growing continuously in the middle or lower levels of the Party in recent years, while in the top levels they have become weaker. This proves that there is no democracy within the Party. In recent years, antireform forces have constantly demanded that Party discipline be strengthened, and have even gone as far as to say that "discipline comes first in the Communist Party." Nevertheless, the "liberalist activities" of prodemocracy forces have become more and more bold. The conflict between Zhao Ziyang and Deng Xiaoping during the student movement in May was in fact an important sign of this boldness and of the further disintegration within the Party. Zhao Ziyang regarded the student movement as a patriotic democratic movement, not a "counterrevolutionary rebellion." It should not be suppressed; instead, there should be dialogue, and the Party should accept reasonable demands. Since Zhao Ziyang was the general secretary of the Central Committee, elected in 1987 by the Thirteenth Congress of the Communist Party, and Deng was not even a member of the Politburo, Zhao should have had power over Deng.

Unfortunately, Zhao was no Gorbachev. He was, however,

a very shrewd bureaucrat. Unlike Hu Yaobang, he had been promoted step by step from the lower levels to the highest level. As a result, he was familiar with all the rules of behavior for officials, and was always cautious, never thoughtless or impulsive. He also knew that Deng and the other Old Men could easily oust him, as they had ousted Hu Yaobang. So where did he get the courage to challenge Deng Xiaoping and run such personal risks?

This move by Zhao was an important signal that the balance of power at the highest levels of the Party, politics, and the military was changing. Zhao must have done serious thinking and consulting with his advisors before he made this move. The conclusion he reached was that if he had followed Deng's orders to kill students, the blame would inevitably fall on him some day. On the other hand, if he refused to take orders, he might sustain temporary serious damage, but there must be many people in the Party and the military who would support him and oppose Deng and the Gang of the Old's attitudes toward the student movement. Furthermore, what Deng did would land him, Yang Shangkun, and Li Peng in a dilemma. The majority of the Party would make a new choice—even if they did not ask him to resume office, they would at least rehabilitate him.

As Zhao expected, right after Deng decided to oust him, Deng ran into a series of difficulties. The first plan was to label Zhao as the leader of the anti-Party clique. Only after they dropped the anti-Party-clique label and lightened the severity of Zhao's crime could they pass the resolution to oust Zhao in the plenary session of the Central Committee. Apparently, Deng's labeling of the student movement and the way he handled Zhao Ziyang were resisted by party secretaries of various provinces, high-ranking military officials, and members of the Central Committee. After these officials were called to Beijing, they were individually persuaded or pressured, and forced to accept Deng's will. Even so, the process was not very smooth.

This has never happened before.

During April and May of 1989, Party committees of the provinces were reluctant to show their support for the Central Committee's handling of the student movement and the issue of martial law. Later, members of the Central Committee and leaders of various organizations in Beijing were forced to show their attitude. After the massacre, all Party officials were forced to take sides. When Mao initiated political campaigns, he had never felt the need to force officials to express their attitudes, for he believed he would win the support of all the officials, or at least the majority of them. There was only one exception. In the last year of his life, he had already lost popular support and was opposed by the majority of the Party officials. That is when he cracked down in the Tiananmen incident of April 1976, and ousted Deng Xiaoping. During those days, officials of all provincial committees and military divisions were holding mass meetings, apparently under pressure from Beijing, with the secretary of the Party committee of each province supporting Mao's decisions. It looked as if everyone agreed with Mao. Six months later, almost all of these people unanimously supported the ousting of the Gang of Four. That was their true feeling.

In the marches headed by students, there were groups composed of the staff members of several departments and bureaus of the General Political Department, the Headquarters of the General Staff, the General Logistics Department, and the central government. Almost all the students of the Party School participated in them. These people were all leaders of provinces and cities. Seventy percent of the ministers and vice-ministers of the central government were sympathetic toward the student movement. Some of them even went to the square to pay their respects to the fasters in the name of their ministries. Officials who were sympathetic to the student movement made up 80 percent of most organizations, including those like the Public Security Department and the Organization Department of the Party. Zhao Ziyang must have derived courage from this fact in his struggle against Deng Xiaoping.

Judging from the wanted list issued after June 4, most of the intellectuals and officials who were wanted or arrested were Party members. Among the five initiators of the Front for a Democratic China, an organization of overseas Chinese announced in July, four were Party members (one has already been dismissed). The only non–Party member was Wuer Kaixi, who was a student leader.

Today, after the massacre, the Communist Party in China is splitting into two parts, although this is not reflected in two different organizations. The Party is deeply split into two opposing political forces. These two opposing forces could still coexist before June 4, but now that the Gang of the Old is in power, it has to wipe out the democratic forces. Under the present circumstances, those who are considered enemies by the Gang of the Old but not yet openly attacked, as well as those who are sympathetic to democracy secretly, are unable to show their strength as yet. However, since the June 4 movement will surely push many who were neutral into the camp of the democratic forces, once the situation calms down and Party members are able to express their opinions openly, the balance of power within the Party will tilt sharply in favor of the democratic forces.

Since the massacre, many Chinese diplomats in the United States, France, Britain, Canada, and Japan, and even one representative sent to participate in the negotiations in Korea, have deserted the Beijing government and sought political asylum in foreign countries. Were it not for concerns about the safety of their families in China and about the difficulty of living alone abroad, the number of diplomats who would openly betray the Beijing government and resign from the Communist Party would be many more.

In the countryside, officials of Party committees and governments of counties openly oppose the Beijing government's forcing peasants to lower their prices for agricultural products, not paying cash for them, and in particular, using the police to force peasants to hand over their grain. Although such officials disagree with the central government, they have to obey its orders. At the same time, they are sympathetic with people's sufferings. Their uncertainty about the country's future, and the feeling that the Beijing government cannot last long, will make more and more Chinese officials do no more than what they absolutely have to do. This will surely leave the already inefficient governments at various levels in a state of semiparalysis. Orders will be disobeyed with increasing frequency. And officials who are sympathetic to the Democracy movement and disagree with the present Party policy will have more opportunities to help those who hate the present government. Since June, many members of the Democracy movement have fled the mainland. This would have been impossible without the support and sympathy of local officials and members of public security agencies.

All the questions and crises of the Communist Party and the Chinese government also exist in the army, only to a more serious degree, and displayed in a more overt fashion. Every time there is a change of personnel and every time there is an adjustment or reorganization of military divisions, the relationships among those in the army who enjoy privileges and the various social factions and organizations undergo a change. The fate of many people is affected by the rise or fall of one individual. Many army officers are dissatisfied with their early retirement. More are dissatisfied with their positions. Amid the complaints of insufficient military spending, there is an ever-increasing trend to use public funds to give banquets or "presents" to high officials. Due to a lack of military funding, soldiers are allowed to engage in business to make up for what they lack. Using military vehicles, ships, and aircraft for the purpose of speculation and racketeering has become widespread, causing further corruption and degeneration of the army.

China is no longer what it was in the thirties and forties, when warlords could bully people as they liked. Local armies are no longer backed up by foreign imperialists. Any head of the army, in order to have a solid base and keep up the living standards of the army, can only continue reform and opening to the outside world. Of course, the possibility of feudal separatist rule and fascist dictatorship by a few conspirators with the military forces cannot be ruled out. Some ambitious military officials have wanted to impose martial law nationally

171

through a military coup and exercise fascist rule. But they would surely meet with popular opposition and be isolated in the world. They could not last long.

Deng Xiaoping is the last one who can still hold the army together to give the appearance of unity. After Deng, anyone who attempts to impose a military dictatorship will face not only a disintegrating country but also an uncontrollable national military force.

CONCLUSION

In one morning in June 1989, the Chinese people suddenly woke up to find that all that they had worked for in the past ten years had disappeared. After the Cultural Revolution ended, intellectuals especially experienced a rare sense of security. Gone were the days when they would be called to a meeting to criticize or struggle against someone, or when they would be the objects of criticism. If you wanted to listen to an old record (if they had not been destroyed), you didn't have to shut the door. If you wanted to listen to the Voice of America, you did not have to be afraid that you would be arrested. You even dared to pass on information you heard from others. People could read the books that had been banned for decades. You could even invite foreigners to have dinner at your house. You could openly express your sympathy for liberals at a meeting "opposing liberalization" organized by the Party committee. You could even express your dissatisfaction with this movement. You knew that phones could be tapped and letters censored, but you paid no attention and you expressed your true feelings nevertheless.

All these freedoms have suddenly disappeared. During the month of May, newspapers and radio and TV stations enjoyed temporary freedom. Students and workers had their organizations for a while. All these have also disappeared. However, one thing has not disappeared. For a few years before May 1989, people on the mainland had been seething with resentment, which could come out at anyone. When someone pushed someone else on a bus, or when a shop assistant was slow, people would burst out in anger—and get an equally impolite response. When the student movement came and people also took to the streets, they discovered that the object of their resentment was none other than the government.

Fifty years ago, when I first became a member of an outer organization of the Communist Party, I was very young, a fourteen-year-old boy who had lived under Japanese rule for eight years and had only a dim understanding and yearning for freedom and light. But it was precisely this dim yearning that brought generations of Chinese who were dissatisfied with the status quo under the flag of the Communist Party. Who would have thought that half a century later we not only did not get what we pursued, but also had to shed blood for it? And the butcher was none other than the symbol of light and truth half a century earlier—the leading organization of the Communist

Party of China. When I was twenty, I never thought that democracy and freedom might be unreachable luxuries for my children. But when I am sixty-four, I have to worry about whether my six-year-old grandson will become a free citizen of China.

Long before June 4, 1989, the Deng Xiaoping regime had already betrayed the Chinese people's hope in it. Deng Xiaoping was willing to give the people limited freedom for only two years—1979 and 1980. Judging from the two campaigns against bourgeois liberalization in 1983 and 1987, Deng Xiaoping never completely changed his own pioneer role in the movement against rightists in 1957.

This, of course, is not a problem of Deng Xiaoping alone. The Chinese people thought that after one Cultural Revolution, those old ones, having tasted the bitter fruit of their own making, would change their minds and return democracy and freedom to the people. Till the end of 1986, when Jiang Jingguo in Taiwan, who had done all kinds of evil during his lifetime, lifted his prohibition on forming parties, publishing newspapers, and martial law, I and many others hoped that Deng Xiaoping would also in his old age make up his mind to return power to the people. I also hoped that Mikhail Gorbachev's political reform in the Soviet Union and changes in Eastern Europe would change the minds of Deng and his clique. But the developments frightened them and made them cling to their power with greater desperation.

When we evaluate the leading organization of the Communist Party, we often neglect one of its features: that it has been through long periods of cruel armed struggles and won its political power with guns. It ruled a country that had no tradition of democracy and was extremely backward and poor. The Soviet Union's military suppression of the Hungarian revolution was conducted at the strong suggestion of the Chinese Communist Party. At that time, Mao Zedong understood the threat democracy constituted for the Communist Party's rule. In China, the June 4 massacre by the leading organization of the Communist Party was not the first one. It was only the first done in the full view of the whole world.

A turning point in China's history has come. The Chinese people are no longer willing to be subject to autocratic rule. And the Chinese Communist Party is having a hard time ruling in the old fashion. Deng Xiaoping and the Gang of the Old discovered that they can no longer be as complacent as Mao was. They are terribly frightened, and that is why they panicked.

During forty years of Communist rule, the Party has constantly made enormous mistakes, and continuous minor errors. Its corruption and incompetence were clear to all. So why did the Chinese people still allow the Party to monopolize all political power? Why didn't the unprecedented Democracy movement of 1989 even mention overthrowing the Communist Party's leadership and the present system of government?

Because until June 4 they still believed in the Communist Party as an abstraction, still hoped that a single man, Deng Xiaoping, could be relied on to reform China. And this was largely because there was no other political force to turn to. They still believed that a majority of the Party members were decent people, that in time corrections could be made, or that the crimes of the past were at least committed out of "good intentions."

The June 4 massacre put an end to all this. It is true that most of the Party members are decent people, but they cannot change the evil deeds of a few on top. No longer will the Party's invocation of its right to speak for "the People" be believed as in the past. What Mao did during the Cultural Revolution was absurd enough. What Deng did was far worse, and he will taste the bitter fruits of his actions far sooner than Mao. He spoke of killing 200,000 people to gain 20 years of peace and stability. But he has massacred only a few thousand, and the whole country showed its revulsion toward him. He wanted to continue autocratic rule, but at last its days have become truly numbered.

Since 1988, it has become a trend to want to flee China. Thousands of young and middle-aged people rushed to foreign embassies in China to get visas. Even though some know that they could only survive abroad by doing manual labor, they nevertheless go. After the June 4 massacre, this trend has become even stronger. Among the Chinese students studying in the United States, the 50 percent who intended to return has dropped to less than 1 percent. Recently, many members and heads of delegations sent abroad have refused to return to China. Because they are afraid that their families will be implicated, they have gone quietly, so they were not reported missing. This poses a difficult question for the Communist Party and the government. Do they dare to send people abroad in the future? In the past, everyone who was going abroad had to go through political inspection. What should they do in the future?

After 1979, the Deng clique could have made the country

more appealing, but they chose to do the opposite. They made the Chinese feel that China is becoming more and more suffocating. The Chinese people have very deep feelings for their motherland, their hometowns, and their loved ones. Still, they are fleeing the mainland as if they were fleeing a sinking ship. This fact is an appropriate comment on the "achievements" of the government headed by the Communist Party.

This ruling body has lost its legality and reason for its existence. Even in their own elaborate manufactured works of propaganda, they could not escape sarcasm. Recently, a movie that shows off the glorious history of the People's Liberation Army, called *The Towering Kunlun Mountain*, was premiered. When scenes of Kuomintang police using water cannons to disperse demonstrating students came onscreen, some among the audience shouted, "They were not nearly as bad as the People's Liberation Army!" Another scene showed Ambassador Leighton Stuart handing American loans to Chiang Kaishek, saying: "This loan cannot be used to suppress people." The audience burst out laughing.

The leadership of the Communist Party has caused China to miss several wonderful historic opportunities. China still remains backward in terms of per-capita gross annual product. It has gone from number 106 to number 128 among all countries in the world. China has even been surpassed by countries like Sri Lanka in terms of per-capita GNP. Due to the Party's mistakes on the questions of population and education, the education level of the Chinese people continues to drop.

Those who fell on the streets of Beijing were in their twenties and thirties. They were born ten or twenty years after the Communist Party took control of the government. Even if they had become true enemies of the Communist Party, the responsibility should rest with the ruling organization. Was it not the parents of these students who welcomed the CCP into Beijing? Did not these students grow up shouting "Long live the Communist Party of China!" and dedicate flowers and songs to the Party with their trust? Why did they become "counterrevolutionary rebels" overnight? From the first day this generation of people was born in China, what happiness have they enjoyed? First they saw and tasted the famine around 1960, followed by lighter but longer-lasting scarcity and extreme lack of material goods in the 1970s. The majority of them suffered from malnutrition, caused entirely by the economic damage by Mao Zedong and his comrades-in-arms, the Gang of the Old. They were also deprived of the opportunity to receive a normal education and the opportunity for employment. Compared with their counterparts in some Third World countries, they had much less space to live in. In China it is very hard to find a lawn on which to play, a tree under which to rest. They drank dirty water, breathed polluted air. But Mao Zedong and the Gang of the Old never paid much attention to these problems.

The Gang of the Old could argue: "But we liberated you from the rule of the Kuomintang and imperialists." True. But under the leadership of the liberators, this generation has had even less freedom than their parents had had when they were young. At that time, the northern warlords and Kuomintang also limited freedom of speech, persecuted opposing political organizations, and murdered their political enemies. But they did not prohibit all private newspapers and independent political organizations. The people could at least

179

hear different opinions. They would not be labeled "elements of the counterrevolutionary rebellion," would not be shot at with dumdum bullets by the government's troops, just for establishing a student union of their own, publishing their own newspapers, or shouting a few anti-Kuomintang slogans in the streets.

This is exactly where the essence of China's problems lies. Mao Zedong said the Chinese people would be content if they were fed and did not starve to death. Deng Xiaoping thought that the Chinese could live a little better than that—as long as they listened to him and made no excessive demands. But both Mao and Deng were adamant about one principle: the people should have no freedom. Deng allowed a certain freedom in attaining material wealth, but political freedom, freedom to extricate themselves from the Party's control, is absolutely not allowed. Even freedom of thought cannot be tolerated. This is why, on April 25, Deng called the student movement in Beijing "counterrevolutionary rebellion" and said, "We must not give in one step." That "one step" refers to democracy.

But what does a China without democracy mean to the world? China's problems are not problems only for itself. The damage done to China by its rulers has turned China into a burden on the world. China should contribute to the development of the world. However, over the past forty years, China's misfortunes are making China a disaster. Due to the Beijing government's corruption and incompetence, China's population has already gotten out of control. It is growing at the rate of more than 20 million each year, and the total has exceeded 1.1 billion. The number of potential unemployed in the countryside is 50 million. For cities, the number is 30 million. The recent political turmoil will make it harder to feed these people. Under the rule of a government that does not keep its promises, that has lost the trust and support of its people, China will become an element of instability in Asia as well as the world. Even a country as small as Vietnam has become a burden to the world by pouring refugees into different countries. It is not hard to imagine when, one day, China's doors are wide open, allowing people to emigrate, what kind of situation it will be.

Sober-minded foreigners saw long ago that the imminent turmoil in China would constitute a threat to foreign business. Last year, an American organization that specialized in feasibility studies for investments named China and the Philippines as among the least safe countries in Asia. A similar organization in Asia announced recently that mainland China has fallen from the third category to the fourth in terms of reliability. Major criminal cases have risen, beginning from 1984, at a rate of 30 to 40 percent a year. Last year, during the height of the inflation, in some large cities the rate was 90 percent. Traveling for business or pleasure is becoming less and less safe. The Public Security Bureau has been unable to curb crime. The success rate for solving cases is decreasing, which encourages more people to commit crime.

Forests and grasslands in China have sustained terrible damage. Now forests are disappearing from the face of the land at the rate of two hectares a minute. Some lakes have disappeared and others are disappearing. Each year, about 500 million tons of earth are washed into the sea. Topsoil that has been destroyed caused what used to be called "the land of Heaven," Sichuan Province, to have droughts, floods, mud-rock flows, or landslide for a number of consecutive years. Random development of high-cost and low-efficiency industries without restraint has made pollution of water and air reach astonishing levels. The government either never started solving the problem of pollution or was ineffective in its efforts. The huge population, together with the damaged environment, will make China one of the foremost contributors to the greenhouse effect in the world. If the government represented by the Gang of the Old were allowed to continue its rule in the same old way, the significance of China to the world could be only natural disasters, famine, and disease, and a threat to the stability and natural environment of the world.

Perhaps some people will say that population crisis and environmental destruction are not just Chinese problems. Many countries have them. But China could have prevented the problems from becoming so serious. Few countries have the high degree of concentration of power that is found in China. If the government were not so corrupt and incompetent, if the officials did not take the lead in undermining population policy and destroying the natural environment, and let people take the country's interest as their own, solutions would be much better and easier.

However, the Chinese people will no longer allow the Gang of the Old to continue manipulating their destiny. The June 4 massacre has broken whatever bound the Chinese people's minds as well as their hands and feet. In the foreseeable future, the main form of struggle will be peaceful and nonviolent. China still does not have a political force ready to replace the present government. But this situation will also make people change the passive attitude in which they have always waited for outside forces to come to their rescue. But as the Communist Party loses control over the whole country and autonomy develops in provinces, cities, and counties, a people's movement will expand from the bottom up. Local officials will pay more and more attention to maintaining and developing the interests of their own localities, and ignore or pretend to comply with Beijing's orders. The levels of economic development, as well as natural conditions, are vastly different in various parts of China, and levels of political consciousness are also different. As a result, some areas will realize political reform through relatively peaceful and stable means, giving people more democracy, while in other areas there might be more turmoil, and they might achieve reform through relatively radical means.

At the same time, pushed by the increasing social crises and waves of popular opposition, the relatively moderate forces within the Communist Party will replace the hard-liners in the government. This, of course, will not be a democratic government. Nor can it immediately rehabilitate the June 4 massacre. But it will quietly make some political concessions to the people. People will gain the kind of limited freedom that they enjoyed before May 1989. But they will not stop there. The appearance of a leader with Gorbachev's style within the Communist Party is not impossible in the future, but the democratic forces will not be satisfied with control by this type of person. The possibility of these forces separating from the Communist Party has been increased by the June 4 massacre. In a country like China where human control overrides legal controls, the death of Deng and some members of the Gang of the Old will exert tremendous influence on the present political situation and speed up all kinds of tendencies that exist.

The Chinese situation is unique and very complicated. It is very hard to predict what will happen. But one thing is certain: The June 4 massacre injured the Democracy movement on the one hand, destroying many of the top scholars and politicians of the past ten years, but it also speeded up all kinds of crises and the people's determination to carry on a more resolute struggle against the Gang of the Old. The few old men like Deng in the Communist Party also did a good thing for China before they bid their eternal good-bye. As a rule, it has been hard for the Chinese to be united. Even when Japanese invaders occupied China for fourteen years, they did not make the Chinese people truly unite. Deng achieved this goal within one day. The June 4 massacre shocked Chinese all over the world and united them into a front of unprecedented strength against the violent rule by force of the Communist Party. Many people of all ages who have not cared about politics for years are now throwing themselves into this movement. The lines of demarcation among left, right, and neutral in politics have disappeared. There are only 6 million residents in Hong Kong. Of these, 1.5 million gathered in the streets to protest against the Chinese government.

Deng would never have guessed, nor would he want to believe, that the public opinion of the whole world is on the side of the "elements of the counterrevolutionary rebellion." On the streets of Paris, in American small towns, and in the mines of Australia, people recall the days of May in Beijing with deep respect and sympathy, and condemn Deng and the Gang of the Old. The Communist Party of China has lost the friendly relations and friendship with other countries that it established over the past few decades. This "accomplishment" of Deng Xiaoping far exceeds what Lin Biao and the Gang of

Four did. Except for Hitler, no ruler in the world has ever been so isolated.

China is approaching the goals that have been fought for over the past hundred years. A democratic new China will be created out of blood.

INDEX

187

Wang Ruoshui, 92
Wang Ruowang, 9, 94
Wang Wei, 144
Wang Weilin, 35
Wang Zhen, xii, 76, 91, 92, 93, 96,
  97, 122
Wan Li, 39, 52–53, 55, 93, 102, 106
Wei Guoqing, 88
Wei Jingsheng, 6–7, 25, 77, 87
Welfare Committee of the
  Handicapped, 12
West, trade with, 155
Western thought, people's interest in,
  148
word-of-mouth political news, 147
worker actions, 160–61, 162
World Economic Herald, 18*n*
Writers' Association, 33
Wuer Kaixi, 13, 19, 29, 35, 49–50,
  51, 169

Xiang Nang, 94
Xiao Bin, 126–28
Xinhua News Agency, 33, 57
Xi Zhongxun, 106

Yan Baohang, 106
Yang Shangkun, xii, 96, 100, 106,
  107
  Democracy movement of 1989, 15,
    42, 43
  Hu Yaobang's memorial, 13, 14
  Zhao Ziyang, denunciation of, 38
Yan Jiaqi, 26, 53, 129
Yan Mingfu, 49, 50–51, 106–7
Yao Yilin, xii, xiii, 91, 103
Ye Jianying, 72, 80
Ye Wenfu, 133

Yin Zhenggao, 151–52
Yongle (emperor), 68
Yuan Mu, 19, 20, 21, 45, 134–35
Yueyang City protests, 151–52
Yu Guangyuan, 95

Zhang Boli, 8, 11, 13, 23–24
Zhang Gong, 134
Zhang Wuchang, 158–59
Zhao Dajun, 36–37
Zhao Ziyang, xii, 15, 18*n*, 71, 93
  as "conspirator" against
    government, 137, 138–40
  corruption charges against, 20,
    36–37
  Democracy movement of 1989, 40,
    49
  fasting students, meeting with,
    42
  mistakes regarding, 41–42, 105,
    106, 108–9
  support for students, 36–38,
    166–67
  downfall, 36, 38–41, 42, 48–49,
    102–3, 107, 166–68
  general secretary, named as, 99–100
  Gorbachev, meeting with, 40
  Hu Yaobang's downfall, 96, 97–98
  "new authoritarianism" program,
    99, 108
  six-point plan, 39
  Wan Li and, 102
Zheng Yi, 24–25
Zhou Enlai, 70, 90, 101, 103
Zhou Fengsuo, 128
Zhou Yang, 92, 95
Zhou Yongjun, 13
Zhu De, 90

Liu Binyan was a reporter for China's leading paper, the *People's Daily*, in the 1970s and 1980s, and became famous for his searing accounts of corruption in the Communist Party. Today he is one of the most revered figures in China. His autobiography will be published by Pantheon in the spring of 1990. Ruan Ming was vice-director of the theoretical research office of the Party School of the Central Committee from 1977 to 1982. He is associated at present with Columbia University. Xu Gang is a poet and writer and editor of the Chinese journal *Chinese Writers*. He is currently living in Paris.